Mickey Mahaffey i.   :less
saunterer across our modern-day dilemmas of faith and
faithlessness, who has written a deeply personal and poetic
memoir of his extraordinary life. Once a legendary Appalachian
kid preacher and star athlete, Mahaffey's fall from grace led him
to an agonizing period on the streets, insane asylums, among
shattered families and the dark woods of outcasts, until he began
a journey of healing, literally walking himself back to a state of
redemption. From the Blue Ridge of North Carolina, the hip
streets of Asheville, to the remote canyons of the Sierra Madre in
Mexico, *Whispers of My Blood* unfolds a spellbinding chronicle of
a quest for forgiveness, love, and renewal.

—Jeff Biggers, author of *The United States of Appalachia* and *In
the Sierra Madre*

Mahaffey unflinchingly examines the raw truths of his life,
spilling blood onto the page as he ventures deeper into the
mountains, the canyons, and himself. He writes with grit and
grace about real matters of the heart. In the frozen stillness of
an Appalachian winter and the searing heat of Mexico's Copper
Canyon, he uncovers startling revelations about love, forgiveness,
and the path of an authentic being.

—Will Harlan, Editor-in-Chief, *Blue Ridge Outdoors Magazine*

Whispers of My Blood es un fuerte llamado a la vida, es un mensaje
que es para todos y que se encuentra en todas partes, sinembargo
Mickey llegó hasta aquí para encontrarlo, en la profundidad de
los cañones, en la serenidad de los Tarahumaras.

—Rossana Gonzalez, public relations, friend of the Raramuri

WHISPERS OF
MY BLOOD

For Peter
KORIMA!

Mickey Mahaffey

WHISPERS OF MY BLOOD

Mickey Mahaffey

iUniverse, Inc.
New York   Bloomington

iUniverse books may be ordered through booksellers or by contacting:

iUniverse
1663 Liberty Drive
Bloomington, IN 47403
www.iuniverse.com
1-800-Authors (1-800-288-4677)

Because of the dynamic nature of the Internet, any Web addresses or links contained in this book may have changed since publication and may no longer be valid. The views expressed in this work are solely those of the author and do not necessarily reflect the views of the publisher, and the publisher hereby disclaims any responsibility for them.

ISBN: 978-1-4502-4643-9 (sc)
ISBN: 978-1-4502-4644-6 (ebook)

Printed in the United States of America

iUniverse rev. date: 08/04/2010

This memoir is dedicated to Peggy Mahaffey, my mother
Stephanie, my daughter
and Andy and Jake, my sons
—my family and my most loyal friends

FOREWORD

Hablar de Mickey Mahaffey es hablar de mi alma.

Cuando nos conocimos Mickey (Gringo, como yo le digo) y yo, supe desde el primer momento que estaba iniciando una relación profunda y duradera. Su personalidad abierta, sus ojos que reflejan su alma y su sonrisa brillante fueron solo la puerta para conocer al hombre que alberga la sabiduría de la vida, la fuerza de la naturaleza, la pasión de la entrega.

En muchos sentidos la vida de Mickey es muy particular. Mickey es amigo de los árboles, de los osos, busca su refugio y su sanación en la profundidad de los bosques, de la noche. Y aunque todo esto es emocionante porque guarda tintes de aventura, demuestra sobre todo una voluntad ferrea de permanecer en las raíces, en el centro de la vida.

Esta particularidad en su estilo de vida además de su contacto con los Ráramuris en lo mas profundo de la sierra Tarahumara, ha hecho de Mickey un hombre compasivo, que está dispuesto a entregarse, a proporcionar ayuda, consuelo y consejo para quienes lo hemos necesitado. Creo que todas las personas que lo hemos conocido, tenemos la sensación de que él nos fue enviado de algún lugar mejor, para estar con nosotros en el lugar y momento indicado.

Pero llegar a ser quien Mickey es, ha implicado para él una busqueda incansable para su autoconocimiento, efectuar cambios radicales en su vida, muchas veces permanecer en soledad. Esto es precisamente lo que nos comunica en su libro, la trayectoria hacia la transformación de un hombre que pretende conocer y realizar su mas profunda misión en la vida.

A lo largo de su relato, Mickey nos va llevando de la mano no solo a conocer su vida, sino también el entramado de las complejidades humanas: el dolor, el vacío, las vanas ilusiones; pero también el despertar, la sanación, la alegría.

Más allá de una simple biografía, la vida de Mickey nos demuestra que las respuestas que estamos buscando afuera, están dentro de nosotros mismos. Que en nuestro corazón y en la conexión profunda con nuestras raíces ancestrales, se encuentra la paz, la fortaleza, la sabiduría y la intuición necesaria para ser felices y hacer realidad nuestros más profundos anhelos!

—*Nubia Yesenia Gamboa Rico*
Chihuahua, Mexico
(For English translation, see Afterword)

ACKNOWLEDGMENTS

Jeff Biggers encouraged me through my first four drafts, gave me a master's level education in writing, and grew to be a real friend. I greatly admire his work with the Raramuri and his book, *In the Sierra Madre*. He continues to inspire thousands with his efforts to save the Appalachians from coal mining, as he eloquently expressed in *Reckoning at Eagle Creek*.

Many, many times I sat with Nelda Holder when we were the only citizen representatives, or some would say rabble-rousers, at meetings with local government. She has performed the unenviable task of translating my English to English. She shepherded me to publication like the classy queen mother she is.

Special thanks to Will Harlan, Allie Morris, Reid Chapman, Brian Sarzynski, Greg Mitchell, Stacy MacDonagh, Reid MacHarg, Susie Mosher, David Eckard, Jeff Fobes, Rod Murphy, Rod Personette, and Don Talley.

Special thanks also to Rossana Gonzalez Borja for hosting me with such heartfelt hospitality during the final writing, and to Santiago Gil for my long stay at Hotel San Felipe El Real in the historic center of Chihuahua City.

To the Raramuri, I give my greatest honor—and to all the beautiful people of Chihuahua who have generously contributed to the health and well-being of Gringo Diablo.

Any deficiencies in the writing of this book are certainly no fault of these friends.

CONTENTS

CHAPTER ONE

Sinner In The Hands Of An Angry God

The heavy steel doors at Appalachian Hall slam shut behind me.

"We're required to place you in the locked unit," the nurse explains, "because you're out of control and we don't want you to hurt yourself."

Two orderlies grasp my arms and escort me through the hall to my assigned room. Other patients peer from the doors of their rooms for a viewing of the new arrival. I avert my eyes from their vacant stares and fix my gaze on my shoes, struggling to comprehend why I was forced to remove the laces as soon as I was admitted to the hospital.

My eyes cross and stray from so much alcohol and the surreal glare of fluorescent lights. I grit my teeth like I'm jacked on cocaine while the orderlies methodically strap my ankles and wrists to the bed frame. The nurse uncaps a syringe with perfunctory motions, like I'm just another whacko to contend with in their daily routine, and shoots my butt full of tranquilizers. When they leave the room I writhe against the leather straps with all my might, gasping for breath until I'm dizzy from exhaustion.

In my delirium I'd imagined a safe haven with professional caregivers, a quiet time of convalescence; instead I'm locked behind steel doors like I'm incarcerated in a prison cell. Maybe that's what I deserve. After thirty-nine years, my life is an abysmal failure. I've destroyed two marriages and distressed the lives of my

1

children, Stephanie, Andy, and Jake. My business is bankrupt. The fruit of all my religious seeking, teaching, and preaching has withered on the vine.

Slowly, the sedatives douse the flames of my rage and turn my muscles to mush. My jaws relax and I feel the soreness from clinching my teeth like a bear trap. My muscles twitch and sensations of exhaustion pulse through my arms and legs as I drift in and out of consciousness. I sink into the bed like I'm slipping on an icy slope, near to plunging into the abyss. I plead for the angel of death to please carry me to my grave and lay me down for my eternal rest, the final solution for my troubled brain. Death seems like the only recourse. I've caused enough destruction.

Late in the night I stare wide—eyed at the ceiling, listening to an elderly woman groaning and crying for help, while random images pass through my mind like a drawing I once saw in a college textbook on early American literature when I was studying for the ministry. Jonathan Edwards, the famous Puritan preacher from the eighteenth century, is holding forth an opened Bible at a tent revival–an angry prophet hurling bolts of wrath from the pulpit. The faces of the congregants are contorted with terror; some climb the tent poles to escape the flames of hell licking at their feet.

I see the Reverend Billy Graham standing behind a pulpit that rises high above an immense crowd anxiously awaiting his every word. He raises his long finger in the air like a dagger of accusation, and with his booming voice, promises hellfire and damnation to those who refuse the call to Jesus.

Again, the images shift. I'm a distraught teenager lying facedown on a football field, cramming my mouth full of grass and dirt in a desperate attempt to choke guilt and shame from my soul. I plead for God to forgive sins I can't even name and beg Jesus to love me even though I've failed him so miserably.

I bury my face in the sheets, remembering all the dismal years I'd spent in castigation, the flames of hell always licking at my heels. Since I was a teenager, I'd proclaimed deliverance in the name of Jesus Christ from pulpits across the country, taught and served from house to house, town to town; yet inside, I've remained imprisoned by fear and shame, forever rocking on my heels before the altar of repentance.

In manic swells of uncommon energy I would rant about Jesus and the Bible incessantly, labor like a Trojan, and sleep very little. I'd contract more work than I could possibly complete. Illusions of grandeur would swallow all semblance of reality until my energy ebbed and the black depression would steal into me, the Holy Spirit leaving in search of a more worthy soul. Then, I would avoid speaking the name of Jesus. I'd work listlessly, if at all. My debts would mount and my relationships suffer. Sometimes I was able to pose as a normal person and keep my anguish a lonely secret; other times the depression would pin me to the floor and rip away my disguise.

Forty years in the proverbial wilderness and the path to the Promised Land still eludes me. Now, I'm laid bare and without defense in the hands of an angry god.

As soon as the psychiatrist is assured that the mania has subsided, he grants me permission to leave the locked unit and participate in group therapy. Most of the patients in my circle are young women who've been sexually and emotionally abused. One woman claims she was whacked with a ball bat the minute she popped out of her mother's womb. She describes her sexual abuse at the hands of her uncle and the family's minister, and further reveals that her father called her a lying whore and slapped her repeatedly when she reported their cruelty.

A teenager clutches her throat, her wrists and forearms crisscrossed with scar tissue. She gives her account of being tied to a chair and repeatedly raped in the mouth by some boys in her high school. She gasps for breath between her words, her voice eerie and raspy as she admits that she'd never told her story to anyone until now. Judging by the glint of anger in her eyes, she could rip the heart out of the next man that crosses her path.

Betrayed by fathers, uncles, brothers, preachers, teachers, and neighbors . . . innocence forever shattered . . . children sentenced to life in an emotional prison. As I listen to their heart-wrenching stories I'm confused and angry. Did God in his foreknowledge allow them to be molested when they were incapable of defending themselves and too young to comprehend? Does God permit the abuse or turn his head or sleep while the innocent are destroyed in a holocaust of fear and pain? I hold my face in my hands as deep sobs convulse my body and grief cuts into my gut like a knife.

With my therapist, I begin to relate the memories that have surfaced during group therapy, but she changes the subject and suggests that I focus on childhood impressions of my father. Instantly, a knot of anxiety forms in my throat as I struggle to conjure his image.

When I was a ministerial student at Gardner-Webb College, I preached a revival in a small country church near Asheville. The sanctuary was packed with a lively crowd shouting amen, hallelujah, and thank you Jesus. My mother and father sat at the back of the church. As I preached I kept the needs of the young people in mind, but I was more focused on finding the words that would move my father. When I offered the invitation for the repentant to come to the altar to get born again or rededicate their lives to the Lord, dozens left their seats and rushed to the front of the church.

More and more penitents followed until the entire congregation knelt in prayer, beseeching the Lord for forgiveness. Except my father. I'd prayed fervently for him to come to the Lord that night, yet he had resisted, even to the last man. I wanted him to get saved and release his anger to God instead of lashing out with so much venom at my mother and brother. But he never budged.

When I was a little boy, we went on an outing to the lake. Once, when my father wasn't watching, I ventured into water over my head. I hadn't yet learned how to swim. I slowly sank to the bottom of the lake three times, frantically pushing my body towards the light with my toes, before the lifeguard lifted me to the pier.

The therapist intervenes. "Did you feel like your father had let you down?"

I hesitate, trying to swallow the lump in my throat. "He always supported everything I was involved in, but whenever I was with him I felt like I was always on the verge of drowning, my cries for his intimacy nothing more than bubbles in the water."

My brother and I hid beneath the bed to escape our father's drunken tirades. He was never affectionate with us unless he was drinking, which was never a daily occurrence. But once he'd uncapped a liquor bottle he didn't stop taking slugs until he'd become a bumbling wreck and had terrorized everyone in his path.

One day I brought one of my new black friends to my parents' house. Maybe I should have known better. The minister of youth at our church had already pulled me aside and suggested that my black friend had his own church to attend. When our schools were first integrated in Hendersonville, North Carolina, the students reacted with curiosity about our new schoolmates. As for me, I'd never understood why the black people had to sit on the back seat of the bus or why public places had separate restrooms. The adults were the ones who had problems with it. Like my father.

"I'll never allow a nigger in my house," he screamed, slamming the door in our faces. I was shocked by the intensity of his anger and the depth of his prejudice.

I remember the times he smashed his rod and reel against the rocks when his hook caught beneath them. I stayed on edge whenever we fished, worked on a project, or when we went on family excursions—never knowing when his temper would erupt and the façade of our happiness would shatter like breaking glass.

Suddenly the image of my father fades from my memory, and I can see myself screaming at my wife—her eyes like those of the terrified souls at Jonathan Edwards' tent revival. I've never actually hit a woman, yet the ferocity of my anger can be as devastating as a blow to the face. In the heat of our argument I smashed stacks of dishes against the fireplace, a man berserk. Later the same evening, I carried my Bible out the door and taught a class about the peace of God that passes understanding, and exhorted all to lift their burdens to Jesus.

The extent of my delusion stuns me. I pull at my hair. I want to throw my chair through the window and slash my body with shards of glass, but my eyes catch the silent presence of my therapist and I slump into the chair, out of breath, like I'd been punched in the stomach.

"How many times did I preach against hypocrisy, a word in ancient Greek that literally means a mask worn by an actor in a play?" I stare into the eyes of my therapist. "Now, I see my reflection in the mirror and realize I'm the actor, the poser that has worn the mask."

I'm startled as the realization cuts through the fog like a streak of lightning

"Am I just like my father?" She doesn't respond. She doesn't need to. I know the answer.

As requested by the therapist, I fill out a questionnaire on my family history. Divorce, separation, alcoholism, and poverty mark my ancestry on all sides. I'd never made the connections.

I'm sitting on a couch in the patients' lounge, crying. I just talked on the telephone to Jake, my five-year-old son. He doesn't understand why I'm in the hospital and begs me to come home. I can still see the bewildered look on his face when I rushed to the car to drive to the hospital, drunk, my brain spinning out of control, my eyes bloodshot with madness. Filled with remorse I weep openly, my fists clinched at my side.

An elderly woman with long, olive hair shuffles into the room holding a cup in her hands and heads straight towards me. She sits beside me on the couch and grasps my hands, prying my fingers apart one by one. Her hands are gnarled from arthritis, yet her touch is soft and knowing. Her blue eyes are serene and gentle like the stillness of a mountain lake. She offers her handkerchief for my tears, places her hand on my shoulder, and motions for me to drink from the cup of cool water.

With her hands covering mine, she tells me a story about working in her garden. Alone, she attempted to pick up a large rock wedged in the dirt beside the stone wall encircling her garden plot. When she hefted the rock to her waist, her head began to spin until she fell atop the wall with the rock in her lap. She says she was unable to lift it from her lap or rise to her feet.

"I was in so much pain and very afraid. I pleaded and pleaded for Jesus to help me," she whispers. "Nobody was at the house and I didn't expect anyone. I stayed alone in the country and my neighbors lived on down the road."

She pauses like she's trying to remember the accurate details, and then she clutches my bicep and leans close to my ear. "Suddenly Jesus appeared in my garden, just as real as you and me sitting here right now, and lifted that rock from my lap." Now, her blue eyes are like fire. "And you know something? I wasn't frightened at all. It seemed like the most natural thing for my Lord and Savior to come to me in my time of need. I'd loved my Jesus since I was a little girl in Sunday school, so you can imagine how blessed I was to see him.

"I asked Jesus how I could repay him for performing such a miracle for me, and all he said was, 'Give a man a cup of cold water.'"

"That happened over thirty years ago," she continues. "In all that time I've never understood what he meant until I saw you sitting here crying like that. So that's why I brought you a cup of cold water. Drink all of it. It's a long-awaited gift from Jesus. Let Him carry your burdens, young man."

I stagger out of the next session with my therapist, stunned by the clarity of my memories—like I'm reliving the nightmares of my past in present tense. Since childhood I'd interpreted the Bible to say that I'm to deny my feelings and my emotions because my humanity is corrupt by nature, and that the only thing I can trust is the Bible. I took the words of my Christian teachers literally, poring over the Scriptures day and night, memorizing entire books of the Bible, quoting the verses over and over so that my thoughts stayed fixed on Jesus.

I'd ascribed the haunting feelings that would often surge into my gut to the influences of devil spirits. Many long nights I'd begged for release from my roller-coaster life. How many times had I thought I was inspired by the power of the Holy Spirit to preach and heal, only to plummet into a dark abyss of melancholy and self-abasement? No one tried harder, nor failed more miserably.

And the mystery of *Alice in Wonderland*? Recently, I'd read through some of my old journals and had come across several references to the acute swooning sensations I'd experience when I read or heard any mention of the Alice story. On the only occasion that I ever ate psilocybin mushrooms, I nearly asphyxiated when, in my hallucination, I fell into an upside-down world. I told my therapist all these things, and as I did I suddenly had the memory of Mr. Hoppity dashing across the dirt road in front of my family's house when I was a little boy.

I held a cup of water in my hands as I told the therapist about following Mr. Hoppity across the street to my grandmother and step-grandfather's house. The little rabbit lived in the bogs behind our house. My younger brother and I thought of him as a pet, even though he never allowed us close enough to touch him. We stood spellbound when he scampered through our yard, and yelped when we returned home at night and he appeared in the car lights like he'd been waiting for us.

One morning I followed Mr. Hoppity across the dirt road, enchanted with the chase like a little boy would be, until he disappeared into the shrubs beneath the bay window of my grandparents' house. Perplexed, I waited and waited for him to reappear.

As I described the setting to the therapist, crystal-clear images began to appear in my immediate line of vision like I was watching a movie reel in slow motion: my grandparents' house set in shade beneath the giant oaks, flaming azaleas, lush green grass, clear blue skies, a soft breeze. Through the bay window I could see the curtains rustle and the hint of a shadow. My step-grandfather appeared in the frame, the sunlight flickering in his glasses, motioning for me to come inside the house.

At that point I was unable to mutter another word to the therapist. I could see myself waiting for Mr. Hoppity while terror gripped my body. I clutched the arms of my chair and clinched my teeth like I was helplessly sliding into a dark hole. Despite the promptings of my therapist to continue, my voice was frozen.

I took deep breaths and waited until I was coherent enough to return to the shocking memories.

My grandfather and I sat together on the couch while I told him about Mr. Hoppity disappearing beneath their shrubs. He offered me a piece of candy, all the while promising to help me find my rabbit friend. As I unwrapped the candy he began to stroke my arms and legs, a very gentle grandfather consoling a little boy. He placed my hand on his legs and coaxed me to rub him as he'd done me, and then he unzipped his pants and asked me to reach inside for a surprise.

Confusion overwhelmed me. I wanted to race outside and hide under the shrubs with Mr. Hoppity, yet I was rooted to the couch while adrenalin rushed through my body. He eased his penis from his pants and placed my hand on it. At first I was fascinated by what my grandfather was doing. He'd always been very kind to me and I trusted him, but the look in his eyes had turned dark and desperate.

I shook my head: No, no, no.

Panic rose into my throat. I slowly backed away and told him I was going to search for Mr. Hoppity. He lunged after me, grabbed my arm, and jerked me close to his face.

"Don't you dare tell anyone about this or I will have to punish you," he sternly whispered. I struggled from his grasp and rushed out the door as fast as my little legs would carry me.

My therapist clasped my hand and called out my name. I opened my eyes, unsure of my whereabouts. She seemed far away, like I was viewing her from the bottom of a deep well, yet I could see the light of day above her. I kept flashing back to the man, appearing again and again in different scenarios like I'd returned to him many times. As she pulled me from the bottom of the hole, I lost sight of him and emerged into the light.

Sitting in silence, I stared at the oak trees outside the hospital window; golden, autumn leaves danced in the air. I heard the beeping of a delivery truck backing away from a loading dock. Slowly, I returned to the present. A great relief settled into my body like I'd exorcised some dark incubus that had been eating at me like a cancer.

I'd never told anyone about the incident with my grandfather. I have vague recollections of other encounters, but I can't say for sure. At that tender age I disappeared into a subterranean world, like Alice. My body walked and talked and laughed and cried, but my inner self had remained in the shadows of a dark hole.

In the ensuing days, I contemplate the experience of rising from that dark well and into the light of day. I see the hand of my therapist as a guide on a path towards sanity. Her presence becomes a safe haven where I can bare my soul without feeling threatened or judged—like a priestess to whom I have come with the deepest revelations of my sordid history. One day I tell her, "Isn't it ironic—a former fundamentalist Christian preacher being ministered to by a Jewish social worker."

A new patient sits in a wheelchair outside the office of the head psychiatrist, his eyes dancing with mischief. He appears to be about my age. His pockmarked face and long nose are framed by a shock of disheveled hair. One of his legs is severed above the kneecap. He's staring into the doctor's office, making crazy faces like a little kid, and then he flips his middle finger at the doctor, laughing hysterically like he's having the time of his life. Within minutes two orderlies rush down the hall and roll him behind the steel doors of the locked unit.

Later I see him on the porch outside the hospital, where many of the patients gather to smoke cigarettes. He's promoting his skills as a dream interpreter to an elderly patient who appears willing to submit the details of his dreams to the man's scrutiny. A handful of others gather round to listen.

"My name is Thomas Didymus, the twin brother of Jesus," the man in the wheelchair declares, "one of the few survivors of the early Christian persecutions."

With that outlandish introduction, Thomas Didymus proceeds to offer a lengthy interpretation of the man's dream, interspersing his comments with quotes from Jesus and very liberal interpretations of the Book of Revelations. Thomas makes little sense, but his subject is mesmerized, swallowing every word as if the crazy man in the wheelchair really is the twin brother of Jesus Christ.

When he's done with his analysis, he gives the man a high five. "The only problem with my analysis of your dreams is that I represent the dark side of my brother!" His crazy laughter rings across the porch. One of the nurses peeks out the window to see what the commotion is all about.

Suddenly, his demeanor turns dark and serious. He holds his finger in the air, waiting until he has everyone's full attention. "When you undress yourselves and are not ashamed, and take your clothing and lay it under your feet, like little children, and tread on it—then you will be sons of the Living One and you will have no fear." Without further ado he rolls away in his wheelchair, leaving us all in a state of bewilderment.

During the days, I weep with the sweet, courageous human beings in my therapy group—people who've been forced through a brutal gauntlet with no means of self protection, hardened survivors who humble me and challenge me to a deeper self-honesty. In the evenings, I laugh with Thomas Didymus—real, cleansing laughter like crying. In lucid moments, his words are so profound and timely that I, too, am almost convinced he's Jesus' twin. Soon he becomes a confidante, a genuine listener who prods me to reveal more details of my personal history.

One night while hanging out in the patients' lounge, I tell Thomas stories about playing football on Friday nights at Hendersonville High School, winning two state championships and coming within five points of capturing a third. Four state track championships, with the record for the fastest mile relay in western North Carolina that stood unbroken for years. President of my class for two years, all-conference in football and all-state in track, voted most popular in my senior class, a decent student, and a dedicated hell-raiser.

I describe how I got born again and gave my testimony for Jesus in front of the entire student body at my high school and preached to a full house at First Baptist Church when I was only seventeen. A revival swept through Hendersonville in 1970 and 1971; the churches filled with teenagers on fire for Jesus. We lived 24/7 to preach, witness, study our Bibles, and pray. Hippies for Jesus, with long hair, wooden crosses, pocketfuls of gospel tracts, and Bibles with wide margins filled with scribbled notes and underlined verses.

We wanted to walk on water and heal the sick and set the captives free. Twice when I was a teenager, I hitchhiked from Hendersonville to the West Coast searching for groups of believers from the Jesus Movement in California and Oregon, witnessing on Sunset Strip, preaching on the beaches at Lincoln City and Coos Bay. I traveled with a fellow ministerial student from Gardner-Webb College, where I graduated with a degree in English and religion.

Thomas is laughing so I stop talking, but he urges me to continue. He's rocking back and forth in his wheelchair like he can't wait for me to finish so he can unload the thoughts percolating in his mind.

By the time I'd reached puberty, it was branded into my conscience that I was filled with the rottenness of sin because of Adam and Eve's original transgression, and that salvation in Jesus was my only hope. Sunday after Sunday I'd heard about eternal security—once saved, always saved—yet I always left the services with the indelible impression that I risked going to hell if I didn't walk the straight and narrow.

Once during a revival, the evangelist leaped from the dais onto the communion table, slammed his big black Bible on top of the table, and stood on it with both feet. The entire congregation was aghast. "Stand on the Word," he bellowed, "because the devil is like a roaring lion, seeking whom he may devour." He sounded like the leonine devil himself, nevertheless his point was well taken. After the service I prayed on my knees, confessing every sin I could remember and begging God to not cast me into the lake of fire.

At times I would backslide for a few days or weeks, taking a bite of Adam and Eve's worm-filled apple and embarking on the path that leads to destruction, sinning for the Serpent with the same zeal as I'd performed works of righteousness for Jesus. The picture of Jesus that hung on the wall in my Sunday-school class would stare at me with those piercing eyes that I couldn't escape no matter how I turned in my chair. I lived in dread of facing those eyes at the Great White Throne of Judgment.

"This is perfect!" Thomas bellows. "What a great story—keep going, keep going." He motions his hands like he's trying to pull the words from my mouth.

"Are you making fun of me?"

He shakes his head vigorously and waits for me to continue, his eyes agleam.

After I graduated college, I left the Baptist church because I came to believe that their interpretation of the Bible was watered down from the Scriptures' original intent. The great epiphany came when I was preaching from behind a pulpit on a Sunday morning, stoked with energy, spinning the crowd with my fire and zeal. I raised my hand to iterate a point, and with my hand suspended in the air I realized that at that point I could've led those people to believe anything I wanted. I had them in the palm of my hand.

For the next fifteen years I was an itinerant preacher and teacher loosely affiliated with various independent ministries. I continued to study the Greek translation of the Bible with great intensity, believing that if I dug deep enough, I could uncover the original truth of God's word. I worked as a house painter to pay my way—

refusing to take money for the work of helping people—and taught and preached nearly every night of the week.

By the time I was twenty-five years old, I'd preached the fundamentalist-Christian message from pulpits throughout the USA and in hospitals, rest homes, prisons, summer camps, Sunday-school classes, prayer meetings, living rooms, bars, and on street corners. I had studied ancient Greek for five years, parsed the scriptures of the old manuscripts from Genesis to Revelations, committed whole books of the New Testament to memory, and prayed on my knees until they were worn raw. I had pounded pulpits and admonished thousands to receive the new birth in Jesus Christ or risk eternity in the fire of a devil's hell.

By the eighties, I was an ardent supporter of Ronald Reagan. To fulfill the American Dream had become my driving ambition; the fundamentalist, anthropocentric point of view, as stated in the book of Genesis—that man is to have dominion over the earth, including dominion over women and children—was my life code. I no longer preached in churches. I organized home fellowships, witnessed in the streets, and canvassed for believers door-to-door, spreading the patriarchal message with great zeal.

Thomas claps his hands, saying he'd give me a standing ovation if he still had a leg; then he stares into my eyes like he's gazing beyond my pupils and into the memory links within my brain. He laughs, "You're just a dumb-as-hell, redneck mountain man with tainted blood. That's your main problem. But fear not, my wayward son, I think I have the remedy."

He raises his finger in the air with the same look of mischief as he'd had sitting outside the office of the psychiatrist. Like he'd waited since the first century for the fullness of time, he claims the moment has come for him and me to travel across the USA holding tent revivals.

"You'll do the preaching. We'll tout you as the great Irish evangelist with a message of great hope for these sorry times. And

I'll be the one who rises from the wheelchair to walk again at every service," he announces. "We'll get on the local radio stations and TV and pass out fliers. Thousands will follow you. We'll make millions!"

He gives me a high five and leans towards me in his wheelchair like he's certain I'm ready to sign on the dotted line.

As I leave Appalachian Hall, I view Mt. Pisgah shimmering in the midday sun. October leaves cover the green grass like fire embers, the rich and variegated colors in stark contrast to the drab, artificial light inside the hospital. I descend the steps feeling a sense of freedom like a convict must feel when the bars are opened. I've made immeasurable progress thanks to the twin brother of Jesus, a woman with a cup of water, and a Jewish therapist who had ministered healing to a broken Christian mind.

Yet my giddiness is tempered. I'm walking into the unknown without a guide, a map, or a compass. Will bouts of depression haunt me the rest of my life? Will I again be fooled by the false energy of mania? Am I consigned to a life in and out the loony bin, like Thomas? He'd ridiculed me for submitting to electric shock, but then his features had turned dark, his eyes nearly rolling into the back of his head, his sadness profound, as his own memories of shock therapy, endless hospitals, and mouthfuls of pills overwhelmed him.

"Hey, next time I see my twin brother I'll put in a good word for you!" The raspy voice of Thomas Didymus echoes across the front lawn of the mental hospital, followed by trails of crazy laughter.

CHAPTER TWO

Abraxas

On a frigid morning in January, I sit by the window in Beanstreets Coffeehouse nursing a cup of coffee, staring blankly at the pages of my journal. Gusty winds sweep flurries of snow across the streets of downtown Asheville, pieces of litter flying wildly in the air. Pedestrians sidestep patches of ice, clutching their hats to their heads. A shiver rattles my body despite the warmth and coziness of the café.

Earlier in the morning I'd ventured outdoors for the first time in three days. Struck down by yet another depression, I'd stayed isolated in my apartment, increasingly baffled by the Jekyll-and-Hyde-like nature of bipolar disorder. Only a few weeks ago I'd dared to believe I'd been making significant progress towards recovery. Not to be. Forcing myself from bed at dawn, I'd braved the cold, hoping the icy air would shock the torpor from my body.

Am I at the mercy of God's judgment because of moral failure? Am I just another baby boomer raised in the era of insatiable consumption? Or did I inherit a whacked-out biochemistry, exacerbated by psychic trauma? Was Thomas Didymus right—just a dumb redneck from Hendersonville with bad blood? Whatever the cause, am I accursed for life? I had asked myself the questions in the stillness of the cold dawn and now I record them in my journal, but I have no words to fill in the blanks.

I've committed myself to Appalachian Hall three times now. On top of that, my orthopedic surgeon's attempt to stitch together lacerated strands of ligaments in my shoulder was unsuccessful. There are no ligaments left in the joint, only bone grinding against bone. At times the pain is excruciating, and my stomach refuses painkillers. Your shoulder joint is irreparable, my doctor reports, and you will endure arthritic pain the rest of your life. The only alternatives: an artificial shoulder or a tropical climate.

I have no clue as to how to proceed with my life with these debilities. The thought of throwing myself to the mercy of the welfare system, food stamps, Medicaid, therapy, and subsidized housing sickens me. Without insurance, a shoulder replacement is out of the question. My debts from treatment are staggering. A tropical climate? I can't even imagine it. I think about the woman for whom Jesus lifted the heavy rock from her lap. Her story remains a powerful impression in my mind, yet the weight I carry still pins me to the wall.

I attempt to rub the weariness from my forehead and eyes, suppressing a groan of dejection.

When I open my eyes, I see a man passing by the window outside the café. His head is wrapped in a light-gray scarf; he's wearing a long, olive trench coat and sandals with mismatched socks. He's dancing along the sidewalk playing a bamboo flute, projecting an aura of serenity and contentment, apparently oblivious to the blustery weather.

When he passes from my view, I turn to see if any of the other patrons had seen him. Two businessmen are engrossed in conversation; a teenager sitting in the corner is fast asleep. A woman is spreading Tarot cards across her table preparing for daily readings. Apparently, no one else *had* seen him.

Was it a vision? Am I hallucinating? His salient appearance stays in my mind the rest of the day as if one of the woman's tarot cards had magically come to life right in front of me.

I'm bowled over when I see him later that evening at Vincent's Ear, a local pub in downtown Asheville. We sit back-to-back in the smoke-filled bar while a punk band wails and screams at the establishment. We turn in our chairs at the same moment, and he introduces himself as Dave.

Like he intuitively knows exactly the words I long to hear, he begins to regale me with stories of living with only the material possessions he can fit into his backpack and the joys of living in service to others. He punctuates every avowal with a fit of laughter, like he's having the time of his life and doesn't have a care in the world.

As the night draws to an end, he grabs the bamboo flute and tugs his backpack from beneath the table. As he pulls on his overcoat he invites me to go camping. I say sure, thinking of warm days in springtime, but he hoists his pack and exclaims, "Let's go right now!"

"How the hell can you go camping in the middle of the night in the dead of winter?"

"Just walk out the door!" he shouts.

His words ring in my head for the next two days. I can think of little else. Every morning I return to the café and watch for him and venture to Pritchard Park scanning the streets at every block, listening for the sound of his flute. I awake in the night at the sound of his voice, "Just walk out the door." Such simple words, yet so full of faith and possibilities. For the first time in many months, the grayness begins to clear from my vision and my steps become lighter.

Dave and I walk out of my downtown apartment and hike towards Rattlesnake Lodge in the Blue Ridge Mountains above Asheville. We walk the side of the road for about ten miles until we come to the trailhead that leads to the ruins of the old lodge. As soon as my feet touch the earthen path, I catch a second wind. I want to walk and never stop. As we traverse the sides of the mountains, I shout my favorite Bible verse from Isaiah: "And you shall go forth with joy and be led forth with peace. The mountains and hills shall break forth before you in singing and all the trees of the field shall clap their hands."

During the night a gaggle of turkeys gobble-gobble through our camp while the full moon rises like a ball of fire over the rocky crags. The ancient mountains welcome me home like a prodigal son. Despite sub-zero temperatures, a sleeping bag with a broken zipper and a shoulder still sore as hell from surgery, I walk back to Asheville knowing the window of possibility is wide open.

A few days later we hike the Mountains-to-Sea Trail to the peak of Mt. Pisgah and camp in the cliffs for two nights. On our return to town we pass through the grounds of the Biltmore Estate along the banks of the French Broad River, slogging through the mud on a rainy day. At one point the sun peeks through the clouds and glows in the misty rain, forming a triple rainbow over our path. We pass through the magical archway, enchanted.

When we stop to rest at the confluence of the French Broad and Swannanoa rivers, I recall the word sunesis, the ancient Greek word for understanding, literally translated as the point where two rivers flow together. Is our coming together like the convergence of two rivers that will lead me to a deeper understanding of life, maybe even healing for my depressions and the arthritis in my body? Does the way Dave lives represent a new path for me to follow?

Can I dare just walk out the door and seek my sanity in the wilderness? And what about my children? I have wanted nothing more than to be the intimate father I'd always longed for. I console myself. Maybe help is on the way. I cling to the light I'd seen with the therapist when she helped raise me from the dark hole of oblivion, and I hold tight to the memory of my soul coming to life on the forest path. I etch the impressions in my mind as landmarks of guidance for the coming days.

I awake at exactly 3 a.m. sensing a presence in my room, yet there is no one. I live in a one-room efficiency apartment so there's no place for an intruder to hide. I lie on my back and breathe deeply, perplexed by the realness of someone having entered my bedroom. I gasp aloud as the image of a woman abruptly enters my mindscape. She's young and old at the same instant, exceptionally beautiful and wizened like a reptile. Her face is alight with joy, yet overwrought with a heartrending sadness, her eyes twinkling with delight and aflame with anger.

The figure of the woman is like a mystical appearance, yet when I open my eyes she vanishes. I wait, very still, listening. I'm perplexed, even anxious should the image reappear. I don't know what to make of it. The noise of a late-night reveler rises from the sidewalk and a street sweeper approaches, its caution light blinking into my room—reassuring signs that I'm not hallucinating or turning upside down in Wonderland.

Did I conjure the vision of the strange woman as a result of my recent readings? Since my first stay in the hospital, I've searched the stacks at the local university library for more knowledge of psychology and non-Christian religions. I've filled my room with dozens of books from a used bookstore in town that relate to different approaches to spirituality. After years of restricting my reading to the Bible and books about the Bible, I've been reading like one starving for wholesome food.

When I was in the hospital, Thomas Didymus had encouraged me to read the Gnostic Scriptures from Nag Hammadi, specifically the interpretations that God and the devil, light and dark, and male and female are one and the same—not opposing entities as I'd always believed. At first I'd passed off his comments as more manic ramblings, yet to read the long-buried history of early Christianity astounds me. The revelation of other gospels and writings outside the traditional canon brings new light, a sunesis, a flowing together of streams of thought I'd never considered.

I'd been intrigued by the references to Abraxas in the novel *Demian* by Hermann Hesse, where the character Pistorius claimed that Abraxas is "God and Satan and he contains both the luminous and the dark world." In my research I discovered that Hesse had a lifelong struggle with depression, nervous disorders, and existential confusion.

I was familiar with the word Abraxas as the title of a rock album by Santana, but I'd never understood the quote on the cover, nor did I recognize it as a line from *Demian*: "We stood before it and began to freeze inside from the exertion. We questioned the painting, berated it, made love to it, prayed to it: We called it mother, called it whore and slut, called it our beloved, called it Abraxas."

The revelations are like seismic shock waves through my psyche, yet I still have a nagging wariness of where such thinking might lead and whether I should even consider such radical concepts. Since childhood, I'd been thoroughly indoctrinated to believe the inerrancy of the Bible, and was warned repeatedly that to entertain such heretical notions from profane literature is like eating forbidden fruit.

Regardless of the sources of the vision or the psychological interpretations or religious discernment, the image of the woman is etched in my mind as a symbol of radical change.

First I receive a postcard from a friend who'd been privy to my mental breakdown. She encourages me to join her in Honduras for a time of recuperation.

Then on two separate occasions, I have chance encounters with old friends I haven't seen in several years. Earlier in our lives, I'd convinced them to follow Jesus Christ, and they had remained very committed to Christianity. I share with them the story of my stays in the hospital and my desperate search for relief from pain.

With nearly the same words and questions, they each offer to finance a trip to Honduras if I'm certain it's God's will for my life. I explain that I'm no longer sure of what that even means. I describe the image of the woman I'd seen in my vision and say that I'd been contemplating the meaning of her symbol far more than wrestling with God's plan for my life. Contrary to my expectations, their offers of support still stand.

I leave the snowy mountains of North Carolina and land in a glorified cow pasture in San Pedro Sula, Honduras.

I'm standing waist deep in the cool waters of the Caribbean Sea, surrounded by dozens of Garifuna kids enjoying a respite from the sultry heat of the tropics. The cerulean sky merges as one with the ocean. Fluffy clouds shroud the peak of Calentura Mountain; refreshing winds sway tall palm trees at the edge of the white beaches rimming the bay. Exultant, I shake my arms in the air and shout hallelujah again and again. The kids stare wide-eyed, giggling with their hands held over their mouths. A tall, white, baldheaded man, yelling at the top of his lungs amidst a throng of little children whose skin is black obsidian.

I remember my trepidation when I first ventured to the Garifuna village of Cristales and became friends with these kids and their families. Former West Africans, the Garifuna had been enslaved and transported to the Caribbean over 300 years ago and they now populate the coasts of Belize, Honduras, Guatemala, and Nicaragua. From the moment I'd arrived in Trujillo, I'd been spellbound by their beautiful features and vibrancy of spirit and had set my sights on getting close to them.

Early in my stay, I inquired about the Garifuna from the owner of The Rogues, a thatched-hut bar on the beach, a popular expatriate gathering spot. I'd seen them playing soccer on the beach in the afternoons and watched them in the mornings as they rowed their canoes just beyond the breaks of the waves, commencing a day of fishing and diving for lobster and conch. From the bar I could see the edges of their village, set among coconut palms where dozens of old, weathered canoes were beached in the sand.

I told Billy, the owner of The Rogues, that I was intrigued by the Garifuna and would like to explore their village.

"Whatever you do, don't go into Cristales," Billy growled. "Them sons of bitches will fuck you up and rob you blind. Ain't that right, Charlie?" He turned to one of his buddies sitting at the bar who perfectly fit the bill of the archetypal pirate from the banana republic—black patch over one eye, long scraggly hair, gold earrings, a .44 Magnum strapped around his shoulder in plain view, and a sheaved hunting knife stuck inside one of his boots.

Charlie nodded his head, "You got that right, Billy. Remember that dumb motherfucker with the Peace Corps who thought he was going to save the Garis? He got fucked up on dope and ended up in jail in La Ceiba. As far as I know he's still there."

"He's still there and probably won't get out until hell freezes over." Billy laughed as he shook his finger at me.

"You might be another one of them gringo do-gooders for all I know, but let me tell you something straight up." He leaned across the bar. "The Garifuna ain't nothin' but goddamn niggers. A nigger is a nigger, whether in California or Trujillo. The best use for them is to grind 'em up, make tar out of 'em, and pave the roads. Or fuck their women. They're no good for anything else." The two men roared with laughter.

I bit my tongue as they spewed their bile. Partly because of the .44 Magnum, but mainly I wanted to see Cristales and form my own judgments. So the next day I headed down the beach, empty-handed, wearing only my bathing trunks. When I neared the edge of the village, I spotted a dozen or so Garifuna hanging out under the palm trees. As I moved closer, a group of five men sauntered out to intercept me, several of them carrying machetes.

They gathered around me, laughing and chattering the patois of English, Spanish, and West African. I recognized a few English words, but had no idea the meaning of their talk or their intention. I assumed they were mocking me. Or planning to rough me up. Their bodies were taut with muscle glistening under jet-black skin, like athletes in their prime. Three wore dreadlocks reaching to their hips. Then the shortest guy among them moved in front of me, holding his hand behind his back, his demeanor menacing. A thick scar curved along the side of his face, and he walked with a limp like his hip was out of place.

With his eyes locked on mine, he slowly revealed a smoking spliff of marijuana. "Ganja, mon?" I nearly collapsed to the sand with relief.

The men doubled over with laughter and assured me of their peaceful intent, crying, "Tranquilo, amigo. Tranquilo." They escorted me into the village as a welcomed guest, offering a far greater sense of safety than I had felt at The Rogues. We quickly became friends, even without a common language and with no regard for skin color.

My first morning in Trujillo. While eating breakfast in a local restaurant, an American walks through the door and without hesitation or invitation, sits down at my table. He owns a factory in Trujillo where he employs about forty local Hondurans to handcraft mahogany furniture for his retail stores at various locations in Louisiana. He carries an air of confidence like he's a man-about-town in Trujillo. The Garifuna waiter refers to him as Mister Richard.

After breakfast he drives me to the edge of town along a rutted road barely wider than a footpath, leading to a camp hidden away at the edge of the jungle.

The small log cabins remind me of any typical summer camp in the states, except the grounds are landscaped with lavish gardens of jungle fauna and flora and coconut palms swaying in the sultry air—like a scene from O. Henry's *Cabbages and Kings*. A clatter of bird sound pierces the air and the hum of swarming insects. Exotic reptiles slither through the grass. The river rushes from the top of the mountain and roars along the edge of the campgrounds en route to the Caribbean Sea.

Mister Richard reveals that he had bought the land and constructed the camp as a retreat for members of the Church of Christ when they come to Trujillo on missionary journeys. On our way through town, he'd made a point to show me their local church and had encouraged me to attend, claiming that they do good work for the poor and the oppressed as Jesus commanded, and that the locals—including many Garifuna—are getting saved and baptized as the Lord commanded.

Mister Richard introduces me to a family of seven Hondurans who live at the edge of the camp and serve as caretakers. I am bowled over when he offers to let me stay in one of the cabins for the duration of my stay in Trujillo—free of charge—and whispers that the family will serve me my food for a few lempiras.

The two teenaged brothers orient me to the grounds, agreeing with me that Trujillo is a paradise, but very quickly warning me that the potential for danger is ever present. They lend me a machete and encourage me to keep it beside my bed at night. If you hear strange noises, drag the machete along the wooden floor to let intruders know you have a weapon, they admonish me. Not to mention the place is crawling with scorpions, tarantulas, snakes and every form of lizard imaginable. The boys roll up their shirtsleeves to show me their scars from scorpion bites, reiterating their claims that I need to stay very alert.

I tie my mosquito net over the bunk bed. Camper Dave, in his impeccable foresight, had gifted me with that before I left Asheville. The mosquitoes of North Carolina are dwarfs compared to their kin in Trujillo, which are reputed to be carriers of malaria. I'd already seen several people with facial scars from bouts with the dreaded disease. As the mosquitoes rise into the twilight I crawl into my bed, tighten the netting, and place the machete within arm's reach.

On my second day, Augustin appears at my door with a platter of sliced papaya, watermelon, and pineapple, and asks in broken English what I would like to order for dinner, which he will serve me whenever I say. I deeply appreciate his hospitality; nevertheless, I am taken aback by his gestures of servility. I insist from the onset that I'm very eager to eat with his family beside the fire and get to know them as my friends.

He is as taken aback as I am, never dreaming that an American would sit side by side and eat the same food as his family. In the best Spanish I can muster, I explain to Augustin that they're not my servants. So we make a deal. I buy the food for the family, and we prepare it and eat together. Rufina, Augustin's wife, hears our conversation and enthusiastically nods her approval like she is thrilled by the prospect of a pleasant diversion from her regular routine.

The two sons fail to loose a coconut from the palms with stones, so they shimmy up the tree and throw five to the ground, lop the tops with machetes, and serve them with a straw. As we sip coconut milk, Augustin—beaming with pride—informs me that he and his boys work for Mister Richard at the mahogany factory. It's the most prized job in Trujillo, one of the few dependable jobs within miles. After dinner he shows me the Bible that had been given to him as a new convert to Mister Richard's Church of

Christ, and tells me that he plans to become a preacher and serve his people the bread of life.

Today is May 18, my birthday. My friends at the camp have been preparing my party for weeks with mucho gusto, whispering around the fire circle, looking towards me and giggling. Sitting around the fire in the evenings, we'd been teaching each other all the words in English and Spanish related to birthdays. Several times I'd offered them money to purchase goodies for the party but they had refused, saying that Mister Richard will pay them at the furniture factory on the morning of my birthday, and everything is already taken care of.

At noon, I espy Augustin and his sons slowly approaching the camp, their shoulders slumped, eyes cast towards the ground. Rufina takes one look at her men and knows something is very wrong. She hurriedly stokes the fire to warm a pot of beans and starts hand-patting tortillas. Her face, so lively with anticipation earlier in the morning, is now shadowed by a dark frown.

Augustin tries unsuccessfully to put a good light on their misfortune. There's no money. No paychecks for anyone. Mister Richard never showed. He reports that most of the workers are still waiting outside Mister Richard's office in the event his private airplane finally arrives. I try my best to rally my friends as we eat beans and tortillas, but there's no joy in the camp and no more mention of my birthday party. Later in the evening one of their fellow workers appears at the camp to report that the tension among the furniture makers is mounting.

Three days later I venture into town to see if there have been any new developments at the factory. Still no signs of or word from the boss man. A large group of workers sit on the wall at the edge of the street, idly tracing their machetes through the sand, raising their heads at every passing car. An involuntary shiver shakes my body. Augustin, who had stayed cheerful and upbeat, is now very concerned. He explains that all of the employees live from paycheck to paycheck and says that now hunger is gnawing at their stomachs and that some of their children desperately need medicine. He's fearful of a riot after hearing whispers among the men about setting fire to the office building and the factory.

Two days later, Mister Richard strolls into camp, laughing and joking with the kids and charming the women as he inspects the grounds. He'd finally made payroll and the furniture plant is back in full production. As I watch the man stroll around his property, I ponder what I will say to him. I think how fortunate I'd been to stay at his camp for four months without charge, and I'm grateful for the rich moments I'd shared with Augustin and his family. Yet, I'm deeply angered by the callousness of what he'd done to his workers. My anger gives way to sadness for the plight of humans and the mix of goodness and badness in Mister Richard, and I reflect on my own culpabilities. Let him who is without sin cast the first stone.

We sit under the gazebo with glasses of fresh-squeezed lemonade served by Rufina and her sister. Augustin, who had toured the grounds with Mister Richard, sits across from me with his Bible resting in his lap. He knows how angry I've been at his employer. Maybe to him the Bible is a token of peace. He probes my eyes expectantly, like he's very anxious about the actions I might take. I wonder if any of the employees had stood up to Mister Richard, and if they lost their jobs as a result.

"Things have been pretty rough around Trujillo the last week or so, Mister Richard."

"Yeah, I know. I just couldn't get away from my office in New Orleans. I've been swamped with work," he explains rather flippantly, like he's irritated I brought up the subject.

I paint a picture of the sadness and fear created by his tardy payment plan and the hardships his employees had endured and how we'd had to cancel my birthday party. I say some of the people just couldn't afford anything to eat and were unable to buy vital medicines for their children.

I pause, staring at the ground, struggling to remain calm. I toss a stone towards a long green lizard. It scurries into the shadows beneath the porch of one of the cabins.

"Don't you think it's good for them every now and then? That way they learn to appreciate what a great job they have," Mister Richard breaks the awkward silence with a chuckle, brushing off my remarks like a noisome mosquito.

I look into Mister Richard's eyes. I see him being lowered into the baptismal waters at the Church of Christ and being raised to newness of life as the Lord commanded. I hear Rufina weeping as she comforts her youngest son during an epileptic seizure. Augustin, Mister Richard's brother in Christ, had no money to buy the medicine that keeps his son's attacks at bay.

I refuse to shake his hand as he rises to leave, and I abruptly walk away, my disgust apparent.

Nearing the end of my time in Trujillo, I become privy to the news that two retirees from Connecticut had purchased a fourteen-year-old girl from her Garifuna family to possess as their sex toy. One day I see them at The Rogues, lounging on the beach with glasses of rum, leering at the girl as she plays at the edge of the surf. I resist confronting the men openly and opt to report their actions to a Peace Corps worker from Trinidad, who in turn relays the news to the local Catholic priest.

A few days later while resting in my cabin, I hear a truck approaching the campground. In four months I'd never seen a vehicle come into the camp. Adrenalin rushes into my gut. Through the screened window, I watch as the truck pulls into view with eight fully armed soldiers filling the bed.

They drive directly to my cabin, surround it, and commence firing their guns into the trees along the riverbank. The commandante approaches my door like he'd known exactly where

I stay, and demands to search the cabin. He checks my passport and visa and pokes around my belongings with his rifle amidst the racket of guns exploding, the sounds echoing up and down the river and through the jungle.

I have nothing to hide from the authorities, yet my knees are trembling from the sounds of the guns and the derisive laughter of the officers. I fear that I'm about to tragically peer into the dark side of the banana republic. I'd seen a few gringo tourists over the months of my visit, but as far as I know the only Americans I could possibly turn to for help are the guys at The Rogues. I quickly conclude that I'd rather deal with rogue policias.

When the commandante is satisfied that he has nothing to pin on me, he orders his men into the truck and they leave without further ado. I collapse onto my bed.

I relate what happened to a guy from Austria who'd been living in Trujillo for five years. In his opinion, I'm a very lucky gringo. He claims the priest is a puppet of the local government, and that the two debauchos who bought the little girl are very wealthy and therefore their voices are much heeded by the authorities. "Normally, the soldiers would have planted a bag of cocaine in your cabin and arrested you on the spot, and left you in the local prison to rot. You are very, very lucky to get a wake-up call; the next time could be much worse. If I were you, I'd leave Trujillo as soon as possible," he sternly warns.

When I report the events to my Garifuna friends in Cristales, they threaten to torch the house of the men from Connecticut and rough up the father who had traded his little girl for money. After many entreaties, they agree to at least wait until I leave Trujillo.

I head out of Trujillo on the bus to San Pedro Sula for my flight home, contemplating the vision of the mysterious woman I'd experienced before leaving Asheville, and how the land and people of Trujillo had manifested her personality in exact replica. I consider the stark contrast between one of my Garifuna friends, a deaf-mute, and the debauched men from Connecticut.

One day, after walking on the beach about two miles from the center of Trujillo, it had suddenly dawned on me that I'd left my leather carrying bag—containing my passport, return plane ticket, money, and my journal—lying on a bench in the central plaza.

Earlier that day I had sat on the bench with my deaf-mute friend. He always approached me with excited grunts and groans, motioning that he wanted to join me. I bought him some juice or a soft drink and we sat in silence, occasionally nodding and smiling at each other. We were unable to communicate with words, yet his company was always pleasant. I was certain I'd left the bag sitting on the bench, and even more sure that in this land of desperate poverty, the bag would be long gone.

I climbed the steps leading up the hill from the beach and walked straight to the park, dreading the moment when I would have to accept that my belongings were lost because of my negligence. My deaf-mute friend was sitting right where I'd left him over three hours earlier. He was clutching my bag to his chest with both hands. When he saw me approaching he held it in the air, grinning from ear to ear and grunting with excitement. Nothing was missing from the bag.

A gentleman who plays chess in el centro and had observed our interaction, reported that the deaf-mute hadn't moved from the bench since I left, and that when several men had tried to wrench the bag from him he'd growled like a madman and scared them away.

Honduras, a harsh and cruel, yet merciful land. Exotic, breathtaking beauty interlaced with death and desperation. Sultry, moon-glow jungles aswarm with malaria-ridden mosquitoes. A simple joy manifest among the poorest of the inhabitants whose guts are gnawed with hunger. So many men so kind and joyful when sober, converted to crazed hoodlums by cocaine, swinging razor-honed machetes. The men at The Rogues, the child molesters, Mister Richard, juxtaposed with Augustin, Rufina, and all the sweet children.

One morning the songs of the howler monkeys awakened me with a start. I eased over the side of the bed, scrutinizing the floor for scorpions, and walked onto the porch with lizards scurrying for cover. I ventured into an open field draped in the soft, ethereal glow of moonlight fading into dawn. Palm fronds danced in the morning breezes high atop their long trunks. The feel of the cool air on my bare torso lifted my spirits into wakeful attention, and my senses flooded with emotion. Laughing tears streamed down my cheeks. In the voices of the monkeys I heard an unearthly sound of joy tempered by the fire of grief and sadness, like a reflection of the land and its people and the mysterious woman of my dream.

As we enter the outskirts of San Pedro Sula, the bus pulls to the side of the road. I wait for the vendors to come onboard selling tacos and sweet bread like at the other stops, but after some excited chatter at the front, all the passengers exit the bus one by one until I'm the only one remaining. Finally the driver turns to inform me that the bus is broken down, and that I will have to find another way into San Pedro Sula.

I begin walking the side of the road, scrambling to gather my senses. All I can see in every direction are row upon row of cardboard and plastic shacks, and throngs of people mostly dressed in rags and pitifully dirty. Many of them take notice as the white man with a backpack and bags filled with gifts passes by. No buses pass, and all the taxi drivers ignore me. I can see the high-rises of the city in the distance, so I keep walking.

Three teenagers hustle up an embankment and stride beside me. One is carrying a heavy stick held against the side of his leg like he's ready to draw. More join them until a dozen or so kids are swarming me, laughing and picking at my backpack. Two of them grab the handbags and disappear into the slums, hotly pursued by several others. Some are trying to unzip my backpack's side pockets. The ringleader, a heavyset girl of about fifteen, obstructs my path with a machete pointing at my throat, so that I'm forced to stop. She's laughing and telling me what bad luck I'm having. Malo suerte, gringo.

A patrol car passes by and the girl lowers the machete. The cop gazes our way but keeps on moving. I'm on my own against a throng of teenagers who live in a constant state of desperation. At the top of my pack is a plastic bag with my money, passport and plane ticket. They pocket all the money and toss my papers to the ground.

Fueled by sheer adrenalin, I snatch a stick from a little kid at my side and begin swinging furiously, making sure to not make contact yet leaving no doubt in their minds that I'm willing and able. I'm convinced they've seen scarier people in their lifetimes, but I project enough strength to scatter them into the shantytown. As I snatch my legal documents from the ground, a tiny Honduran man and his even tinier wife pull their car to the side of the road, unsolicited, and offer me a ride into the city. Angels of mercy in a human hell.

Penniless in San Pedro Sula, I pray my way through the night as I wander the streets of the inner city assuming I will be accosted at any second. After the close call with the police in Trujillo and the encounter with the gang of teens, my nerves are on edge. As soon as dawn breaks, I breathe a sigh of relief and commence walking about eight miles to the airport.

Instead of a direct flight to Miami, my flight is rerouted to El Salvador and then to Belize. An American in a business suit enters the cabin at the airport in Belize City and takes the only vacant seat, beside me.

I stifle a groan and cover my head, feigning sleep. Americanism has left a sour taste in my mouth. One afternoon when I was hanging out in Cristales at Mario's Restaurant, a Garifuna man whom I'd never seen chose me as a scapegoat for all the misery that rich white people had perpetrated on his people. He bit into a shard of concrete block so that I would never forget how the avarice of white men had chewed up his people, first by enslaving them in Africa and then perpetrating violence upon them during the Contra Wars in the name of peacekeeping. He also mentioned the name of Mister Richard and the incident on payday. Lips cracked and bleeding from chewing concrete, he ended up embracing me like a brother.

I recognize the accent of the man sitting beside me. He's from Pelzer, South Carolina, where my father was born and raised and where much of my family still lives—and he's acquainted with them. I tell the story about the gang of kids robbing the last of my money. He immediately pulls out his wallet and offers me fifty dollars so I can afford to eat on the way home. With a deep sigh of relief, I offer to mail the money to Pelzer as soon as I arrive in Asheville. He says he comes to Asheville on business on a regular basis and will drop in Beanstreets and ask for me, all the while assuring me that he's not worried about getting the fifty dollars back.

I sit in Beanstreets café in Asheville enjoying my first sense of security in four months. No machetes, no police with uzis and shotguns, no menacing gangs wandering the streets, no scorpions or tarantulas. One morning about two weeks after my return, the man from Pelzer appears in the café. I hand him fifty dollars.

CHAPTER THREE

Rite Of Passage On The Outer Banks

Camper Dave sits atop his backpack, watching seabirds kiting towards us like wilderness scouts sent to determine the intent of these intruders into their sanctuary. The tip of the sun seethes at the horizon, firing rays of incandescence through the cobalt sky. Shadow spreads across the sand dunes while straw grass twirls in the soft breezes. I lie on the beach and prop my head against my backpack, feeling the tremors of the tiny island as high tide pounds the shoreline.

Dave appears to be refreshed from the day's effort, no trace of fatigue showing on his face. As for me, my heavy pack has taken its toll. My muscles throb and twitch in the still-hot sand. At the onset, I was awkward with my steps and discomfited by the weight and timid in front of so many people. We'd commenced walking from beneath the fishing pier at Kitty Hawk on North Carolina's Outer Banks, wending our way through throngs of sunbathers, fishing lines, hotels, and condominiums. Heads tied with turbans, wearing long-sleeved shirts and pants, carrying food, water, and gear, we'd walked all day in the scorching July sun.

Now we rest on the deserted beaches of Pea Island National Seashore, where the barrier islands are so narrow a good arm could throw a rock from the shoreline of the Atlantic Ocean to the wide waters of the Pamlico Sound.

All day I'd thought about the weight of material possessions and how seduced and addicted to the consumer value system our culture really is. Earlier in the day I'd watched the incoming tide inching towards a kid's sandcastle until the water swallowed it without a trace. One surge of the ocean, and the American Dream dissolves in front of our eyes. I recall the young Garifuna man bowed at my feet, gnawing on concrete to demonstrate the far-reaching effects of unmitigated consumerism in the United States.

At the other extreme, Dave's carrying the entirety of his earthly possessions in a small backpack: a sleeping bag, poncho, mosquito net, one cook pot, a knife and whetstone, spoon, cup, a ball of string and a few toiletries—toothpaste, toothbrush, and floss. With aching shoulders I'd commented how much I needed to lighten my load, and he'd bemoaned his load as well, but his pack is tight and half the size of mine. "You just don't need very much, really. What a relief to learn to live with just the basics. Life is pretty simple really; we're the ones who make it so damned complicated and confusing."

I remember coming to the Outer Banks with my parents when my brother and I were teenagers. We'd whined about the total absence of entertainment, feeling like we'd been banished to a remote and desolate island, like Robinson Crusoe. In those days the beaches were all but deserted, with only a few small motels, restaurants and souvenir shops dotting the shoreline.

Now, hotels and condos rim the beaches all the way to the northern and southern horizons, the high-rise buildings shimmering in the haze like phantasms. Juxtaposed with the wild ocean, stunning beaches and an immense blue sky, the manmade constructs appear garish and incongruous—diabolic intrusions into the sanctity of wilderness. I shudder to remember that I'd been an ardent Reagan Republican, voting for development and prosperity in the name of God and the American way of life.

I'd believed beyond a shadow of a doubt that our country is blessed and holier than any other place on earth, that Americans are God's chosen people. I vividly recall hearing Billy Graham make those claims about the USA when he preached at my home church in Hendersonville, as he was extolling the virtues of his friend President Richard Nixon. As has happened so many times since my first stay in the mental hospital, I'm baffled by the extent of my blindness, and how gullible I'd been to believe my Christian teachers.

I spread the contents of my pack on my poncho and carefully consider the value of each item. I certainly don't need four pairs of socks and underwear, two pairs of shoes, or three books and two notebooks. The unwritten word unfolding before my eyes is too rich to escape into the printed word of others' experiences. On second thought, I retrieve one notebook from the discard pile to record our journey. I'd faithfully kept a journal since high school. In reading the journals over the past months, I'd recognized many of the patterns of my mania and depression, which has assisted me in understanding the root causes of my maladies. Of all the accounts in my diaries, I have the distinct sense this experience will be worth remembering the rest of my life.

"I wondered how long it would take to prune down that backpack," Dave says, chuckling. "Weight is everything when covering twenty or twenty-five miles a day by foot."

He cautions that mental and emotional weight is often more difficult to cast aside than a few material possessions. He'd already told me about his years as a "gutter drunk," and the meaninglessness of the existence he'd lived as part-owner of his family's seafood business in Kitty Hawk. He'd bought a nice house and car and was renowned around the Outer Banks as a serious party man. Finally, sick of living like a reprobate, he quit drinking and camped in the yard outside his house for months until he'd sufficiently recovered from a life built around alcohol.

Then he sold his house, paying off the mortgage, and gradually whittled down his earthly possessions to the few things he could fit into a small backpack.

"I'd faced up to many of my egocentricities when I quit drinking, but when I first began living outdoors and walking long distance, every unresolved issue I'd ever had came back to haunt me, along with my insatiable cravings for and attachments to the conveniences of the modern world," he confides.

"I quickly discovered how pitifully lost in illusion I was. As I went along, I learned to give my memories and crazy thoughts free rein, letting them pass through my mind unfiltered, giving them no value judgment of good or bad, or right or wrong. Like with dreams, our darkest thoughts can lead to a truer inner knowledge if we can break free from their subjective power."

He hesitates, scanning the water like he's fishing for the choicest words to express what he'd pondered for so long in solitude. "If I become obsessed with my fear of failure, or my weaknesses as a human being, then I'm in trouble. The accuser in my brain starts wagging the finger at everything I do and say until I think I'm the sorriest human alive."

Dave breaks into laughter as he rises from the sand and does a jig to the waters edge, playing the flute. "When I'm weighted down with fears, or strung out on the incessant accusations in my brain, I chant and dance until they evaporate. Then I think, what was I so worried about?"

I rise from the sand, refreshed by cool air and energized by the timely words from Dave. "The accuser," I whisper. "I know the accuser."

From birth I'd heard that God judges all my actions and that punishment is the reward for my every misdeed. In the brilliant light of the Outer Banks, I begin to realize that I'd lived a thousand illusions separate from reality, lost in the proverbial wilderness for forty years, the whole time thinking I was on the path of righteousness. I know it will be more difficult to haul that hubris to the burning ground than to leave behind some clothes and books.

We rest on the beaches near Rodanthe. We'd survived a hellish night of mosquitoes and no-see-ums, furious wind, hard rain, thunder and lightning—one of the most miserable nights of my life. We'd rushed into a crater-like recess between two sand dunes and attempted to string up our mosquito net and cover it with ponchos. Swarms of mosquitoes attacked our faces and hands while we worked; the wind whipped the ponchos from our grasp before we could secure them. In the night, soaking wet and itching like a flea-bitten dog, I had decided to call it quits and head to the mountains at sunrise.

Once during the night, I had checked to see how Dave was faring. He was sound asleep while a dozen mosquitoes feasted on his face and forehead, seemingly as content with the evening as he was. That really freaked me out.

But now, in the early moments of dawn, a school of dolphins dive through the swells of the placid seas and squawking seagulls glide through cloudless skies, heralding the promise of a new day. Legions of sandpipers scurry up the beach to escape the crashing waves and then scamper after the receding water, pecking for morning delicacies. Crabs rush in and out of subterranean hideaways. Exhilaration surges through me as the orange sun peaks over the horizon. Humbled by the force of the elements, inspired by the awesome power of water life, I'm ready to continue our trek for a few more days.

In Honduras, I'd caught glimpses of what life can be without pain and emotional turmoil. I still shudder when I remember the sterile halls of the mental hospital, and all the destruction I'd caused. Only a few months ago I was strapped to a hospital bed, to restrain me from hurting others or myself. I can't return to those morbid days, and I don't want to lose the ground I gained in Honduras. As insane as this path appears—the way Camper Dave lives—I'm beginning to think it's a viable way to nurse myself back to health. And maybe my only recourse.

However, to do so means to be more and more separated from my family and less and less in a position to support them. I want to find my way back to a close relationship with my children, but I'm not worth a damn to them the way I've been. I explain my dilemma to Dave and tell him that I want to set aside all other considerations for a time and live intimately with nature.

"But I need to go to Richmond and talk to my kids before I make such a radical move," I confide.

"Well then, let's go to Richmond!" Dave shouts, like it's as good a choice as any.

"How would we get there?"

"Walk, of course!"

We'd considered walking all the way to Florida, or turning west at the southern tip of the Outer Banks and walking to Asheville. So much for plans. Nearing the elbow of the Outer Banks at Cape Hatteras, where the barrier islands veer to the southwest, we make a U-turn in the sand and head north towards Virginia Beach.

We walk until the last rays of the sun fan across the sky, the reflected light dancing like fire in the rambunctious ocean. We gather enough scrap pieces of driftwood from among the dunes to make a campfire and cook oatmeal and boil coffee. We string up the mosquito net and pile sand at the edges as a barricade to fend off mosquitoes. Just as the moon emerges from the tranquil waters, I fall into a deep, restful sleep and don't stir until dawn.

I awake as the sun arises over the Atlantic Ocean and the mystical dolphins sail through the swells close to shore. Buoyed by the heady power of the pristine beaches, I'm thinking our short hike could turn into a much longer excursion—like the birds must feel when they're moved to migration.

We figure it will take us three days to reach the southern edge of Virginia Beach. There's no potable water, no civilization in between here and there. We'll have to maintain a swift pace and drink our water sparingly. We're toting two gallons apiece and the water is already heavy in our packs and tepid from the extreme heat. Dave had sold a bag full of sea glass he'd collected on the beaches at a trinket shop when we passed through Kitty Hawk. We bought a jar of peanut butter and a loaf of bread, and foraged a sack of rosebuds from a garden near the beach, and a handful of figs.

North of the Corolla township, all signs of human existence fade into an immensity of sand, sky, and water. I have the sense I'm walking in place, suspended in time, in a visionary trance. The humped dunes are rimmed with wild mustard greens and sea oats dancing in the breeze. The fury of high tide is more pronounced on the deserted shores, low tide more gentle, thousands of sea birds more alive and intimate with our journey.

I'm in perfect rhythm with the blood pulsating through my veins and capillaries, flushing my tendons and ligaments with vital fluids. All parts in synchronicity, every single organ vital to the others; the muscles of my thighs and calves relying on the well-being of my feet, hands and arms—all dependent on the intricate balance of my brain and my emotions. Walking with the wind day after day, the sun and moon my constant companions, curling into the warm sand to rest tired throbbing muscles, and saturated with the waters of the ancient ocean.

The vision of the intricate balance of all life flows like new water into the dry riverbeds of my mind. My stifled passions surface like the dolphins soaring from the depths of the sea. My emotions, so long denied, so long suppressed by pain and confusion, erupt from my belly, gushing forth with laughter and tears at the same instant. To feel such relief from pain and dread exceeds all my imaginings. I splash my feet in seawater like a little boy in his first mud puddle, remembering the words Thomas Didymus had quoted in the hospital: "When you undress yourselves and are not ashamed, and take your clothing and lay it under your feet, like little children, and tread on it—then you will be sons of the Living One, and you will have no fear."

Like the moment on the beach at Trujillo, I nearly crumble to the sand at the thought that I have little memory of life without pain.

Dave calls it chanting. That was one of the topics of our first conversation at Vincent's Ear on that magical winter night in downtown Asheville. He claims I'm the first person he'd ever met whose customary form of prayer is speaking in tongues, using the phrase I'd learned in the Bible and through much exposure to charismatic churches.

He'd discovered it spontaneously at a moment when he'd walked solo for a week. The words initially sounded like gibberish, he explains—the nonsensical babblings of the demented—yet the words began to flow like a fountain of water, like they had a life of their own. I tell him that I call speaking in tongues the songs of my emotions or of my spirit that arise from the deepest parts of my psyche.

When I was in high school, a close friend came home from college and excitedly reported his first experience of speaking in tongues. I was intrigued. I'd studied many of the Scriptural references to the phenomenon and had wondered why it was never practiced in my church, since it is written about in the Bible. I'd questioned many of my Christian peers, but they offered generic answers that never satisfied my curiosity. Most of the denominational churches are adamant about the Bible being the Word of God, from Genesis to Revelations, so I'd never understood why they conveniently overlooked certain parts.

My friend gathered a group together and taught us all he'd learned about tongues. He spoke a weird-sounding language aloud and then urged the rest of us to try it. Just start speaking without thinking about formulating the words, and the Holy Spirit will provide the words, he claimed. That's all the instruction he offered.

Everyone was very skeptical and too timid to try it. Except for me. I instantly began to speak in what sounded like a legitimate foreign language. After a few tentative utterances, the words began to flow from my lips spontaneously. I didn't sleep that night. I had no idea what I was doing, but I couldn't stop speaking this new language.

The next morning as I was vacuuming the sanctuary at the church, I sang with all my heart—the strange words echoing across the vaulted ceiling. I was the janitor at First Baptist Church in Hendersonville when I was a senior in high school, as thrilled with the work as if I'd been tapped to be the main preacher. I felt fortunate to serve the Lord in the most menial of jobs, so I worked hard and was a very dependable employee. That morning I was in ecstasy as I worked, wondering what would happened if someone discovered me.

I've never stopped praying with the unknown tongue and no longer attempt to analyze what it is or what effect it is supposed to have. It's a private prayer that gives me a great sense of inner strength and comfort that all things I pray for will be to the greater good. Dave and I agree that critics can say whatever they want.

After our discussion, we drift far apart to walk in our own solitude. I hear him chanting as he pulls ahead of me. The sounds of my own voice reach across the wide expanse of the great ocean.

Suddenly, we reach the southern edge of Virginia Beach only to be confronted by a wide inlet, impossible to cross by foot. Undaunted, Dave approaches a man preparing his boat for a day of fishing. Literally without breaking stride, we hitch a ride on the boat and reach civilization, clean drinking water, and food.

I'm camped behind a hedgerow at The Sacred Heart Cathedral in inner city Richmond, Virginia. Dave is visiting with an old friend, and I haven't seen him in two days. We'd made it all the way to Virginia Beach and then turned inland, walking the roadsides to Richmond. After three days of pure wilderness solitude, the onslaught of noise and traffic and the manic pace of American culture disoriented me. I'd walked barefoot on the beaches, and the sand had worn all the callus from the bottoms of my feet. Traveling on the side of the road left my feet blistered and cut so badly that I could barely walk.

I spend a week waiting for my feet to heal, sleeping each night beside the cathedral, searching dumpsters for food or eating at the homeless shelter. Stephanie and Andy aren't sure what to make of my plan for a new lifestyle. They're accustomed to me as a businessman with money in my pocket for meals at restaurants, movies, and gifts. Now, their Dad is penniless and living in the streets. They're intrigued by my stories of Honduras and are amazed that I'd walked such a long distance on the beaches of the Outer Banks. Still, they're perplexed by the decision I've made.

With change we'd found on the sidewalks and roadsides, Dave and I buy two seats on the city bus that we take to the edge of downtown Richmond where the interstates divide, one heading towards the coast, the other to the south. As we approach the juncture, Dave asks me what I've decided to do. We'd discussed dozens of different possibilities, all of which included us staying in tandem, but when I point south, Dave points towards the coast. We embrace with tears. A car picks up Dave before he even raises his thumb. Within ten minutes I'm in the cab of a truck, headed to the Blue Ridge Parkway with the intention of walking solo to Asheville.

I'm hitchhiking towards the Parkway on the interstate highway at the Virginia/North Carolina state line. A man in a sleek new Audi picks me up and asks, "Where have you come from?"

"I've come from a long, slow walk on the beaches of the Outer Banks of North Carolina with my good friend Camper Dave. We walked all the way to Virginia Beach, walked and hitchhiked from the coast to Richmond where we camped for a week behind the shrubs at Sacred Heart Cathedral in the inner city."

He searches my eyes as if to discern whether I'm lying or not.

"Where are you going?"

"I'm headed to Asheville, North Carolina, on the Blue Ridge Parkway, by foot."

He asks me if I'm crazy. I say, "I was crazy for a long, long time, but I think I'm better now."

"What do you carry with you? Looks like your backpack is pretty light."

"I left Kitty Hawk with a pack full of stuff. After more than 300 miles on foot, I'm down to a poncho, a cook pot, a toothbrush, and a water bottle. And the indispensable mosquito net. I want to travel as light as possible. When walking long distance, weight is everything."

"And you're really going to walk all the way to Asheville?"

"It's over 100 miles from here so I don't know if I'll make it all the way. I'll take it one day at a time, but I'd like to. Nothing has ever done me so good as a long walk."

"What do you have to walk in besides those flip-flops, and why's that plant stuffed under your feet?"

"They're all I have. The straps broke on my sandals so I picked these up along the way. They fit well on my feet, but I don't know how long they'll last. They're pretty worn out. Those are mullein leaves that I use as footpads."

He's incredulous. "Son, I hate to be the one to tell you, but you're still crazy!"

When we reach the entrance to the Parkway, he stops the car and we both get out. We embrace. He says he wishes he could go with me.

In a world moving faster than the hare, I slow my pace to that of the turtle. I commence the long trek towards Asheville pondering the questions the man had asked me: "Where have you come from? Where are you going?"

From the moment Dave and I had commenced our journey from beneath the pier at Kitty Hawk, I'd had the distinct sense that an unseen guide was directing my steps, like a teacher, like my own inner guru in the school of the traveler. In the beginning Dave was my guide, showing me a new and creative way, teaching me the basics of living outdoors, patiently instructing me in the realities of the inevitable inner journey that goes hand-in-hand with the geographical journey. Now, I've trekked some 200 miles across the Blue Ridge Parkway alone, learning to rely on my own resources.

On the Outer Banks, nature roared through my body and mind like some wild, ancient prophet, toppling all the coveted idols of my religious past. Now I have more of a sense of what it means to listen directly to the whispers of my own blood and to rely on my instincts undiluted by mediators.

In the mental hospital I'd been diagnosed with a borderline personality disorder. The Greek word for salvation literally means wholeness. Could Jesus have been talking about the integration of personality when he said he came to bring salvation to the lost? Helping broken souls find a way to a personality in order?

Misty twilight veils the light of day. Evening dew falls softly into the swaying arms of the straw grass as the ten-point buck stares into my eyes, never flinching. I lie perfectly still on my sleeping bag.

A perceptible hush pervades the pastoral glen and the deep forest rimming the perimeter, as if all of life is observing our encounter.

The massive deer suddenly darts across the meadow with bounding leaps, swishing through the tall grass. I can hear his wheezing breath and see the glow of his white flag-tail. In silhouette at the upper end of the meadow, the power of his palpable presence emanates thoughout the meadow. Then, he bounds into the depths of the dark forest. I catch my breath, as awed by our intimate encounter as I had been by the dolphins on the Outer Banks. An exchange of energy, an ineffable connection between his blood and mine. I drift into sleep never having felt so much a part of all the living, breathing miracles of creation.

Walking alone along the crests of the Blue Ridge Mountains, I hear the call of the wild enticing me to enter her domain. The polar currents of life and death, solar and lunar energy, of flesh and spirit, of heaven and earth are merging as one in my conceptual thinking. And manic depression. I've walked through the cycles, with sufficient time to observe my thought processes and to see clearly how my emotions have controlled my life.

I'm learning to accept my condition, to flow with it, to adjust my lifestyle according to the times of depression and the times of great energy. In the solitude of the camp, I can hear the voices of my blood pleading for me to accept myself as I am. Beside the campfire, depression instructs me in the ways of silence and stillness. Sadness teaches me quiet contemplation. With a deeper awareness of and a broader objectivity towards my condition, the power of the extremes is greatly diminished.

The lonely mountain peaks, soaked with rain. The rhythm of walking with my bare feet in direct contact with the living earth. I'd never been so inspired to live each moment one breath at a time. Dawn light. A giant red-tailed hawk soars across the mountainsides on the rise of the morning thermals. I catch a glimpse of eternity through her wings. Was I taught to fear the wilderness, to shun nature as the realm of witches and pagan religions? Was I indoctrinated with the belief that man is to have dominion over the earth, including all plant and animal life, other races of people, over women and children?

Long before dawn, thunder and lightning, strong winds, and a deluge of rain awaken me. I gather my things and walk into the dense clouds at an altitude of 6,000 feet. A herd of deer scampers across the tops of the cliffs above the road. I can't see them, but I hear their wheezing breath and the clatter of hoofbeats across the boulders. Are they going to trample me into the pavement— unable to see me through the driving rain and dense fog—or unloose an avalanche of rocks from the sides of the mountains? I accept the threat as a necessary part of life, far more natural than the threat of cars and trucks zooming along the roads like post-apocalyptic demons.

I walk into Asheville barefoot, carrying a clear vision of the path I want to follow. Is it another manic delusion? Or the whispers of my blood coaxing me towards a better way? Regardless, I can't return to my former ways. Never again will I be strapped to a bed in a mental hospital. I must do whatever it takes, even if it means that I'm separated from my family and unable to support them. I'll find a way, even if it takes me the rest of my life.

The most valuable lesson I'd learned on my long journey?

One day while walking along the shoreline, I asked Dave if he calls himself a Christian, a Buddhist, a Gnostic, a wanderer, gypsy, hobo, or what?

"I just call myself David."

CHAPTER FOUR

Pilgrim at Badger Creek

After dark, I leave the center of town and walk to my home at Badger Creek.

As soon as I'm assured no one is watching, I veer from the sidewalk and cut through a tangle of undergrowth until I find the trail that runs along the creek. Patches of snow sparkle in the moonlight. Tiny icicles drape the rocks at the edge of the brook. I choose my steps carefully on the muddy path, my thoughts on a fire and a warm sleeping bag.

As I approach the hovel, I hesitate to see if anyone is inside. For the unsuspecting, there's only a random pile of brush stacked against a large boulder at the bottom of the ravine. Houses stand nearby and a four-lane road runs at the top of the ravine, but the hut sits out of view. Given all the efforts by the City of Asheville to chase the homeless out of the bushes, it's amazing we haven't been discovered. So far so good. We have a pristine hideaway among thriving wildlife and a creek gurgling across a bed of rocks.

I named the camp after my friend Badger, a dedicated, home-free soul who'd lived here for a few years. When he moved away, he bequeathed the spot to me. I napped under the lean-to on the day Badger told me about it. When I awoke snow was falling like crazy, so I rushed outside to gather firewood and stayed for the night. The next day I made some repairs in the roof, cleaned up a little, and have lived here since.

I sniff the air for smoke, but I don't smell anything. Wait ... I spot a faint glow through the pile of brush. I lift the flap covering the entrance and peek inside. Flute John is sitting cross-legged, staring into a small fire. I crawl through the opening and comfort myself close to the heat. Enough room for three to stretch out in sleeping bags and a fire pit in the corner against the arching boulder, like a primitive's cave yet to be discovered by the industrialized world.

Flute John is one of the home-free souls living in the woods in and around Asheville. Camper Dave coined the phrase "home-free" to mark a distinction between our manner of living outdoors from the generic concept of the homeless, and to underline that we do so by choice. Many of the truly homeless are in desperate straits. The camp at Badger Creek, or the others we've made at Rattlesnake Lodge, the Summit, Moore's Cove, or Blackberry Hill, are homes for us as much as any houses we've ever lived in.

We don't beg or panhandle, nor do we stay in the shelters. We eat leftovers and giveaways and rummage through dumpsters and forage the woods for greens and berries. We join the free meals and potluck dinners that are common around our community, where food and generosity abound.

I've lived around Flute John for a while and I've never heard of him sleeping inside. Occasionally he stays at Badger Creek, but more often he camps alone. He stays in the woods and sings and plays ancient Gaelic ballads on his flute. When John is satisfied with a new piece of music, he ventures into downtown to play in the streets or in pubs, music shops, cafés, on back porches, and at the Church of the Advocate on Sunday afternoon. He's twenty years old and knows the way for his life. He's a good man around the campfire, and his flute is peaceful in the streets.

I pour John and me a cup of boiling water for instant coffee and split a candy bar I bought with the change I'd found while picking up litter earlier in the day. He points to a loaf of bread lying on a flat rock at the edge of the fire pit. Says he'd found it in a dumpster behind a bakery.

"Like Camper Dave always says, 'Everything you need is on the side of the road!'" John laughs.

"The basics are, that's for sure. When I leave camp in the morning, I never know what I'm going to eat, or when, what or how. But by the time I return to camp in the evening I've eaten well. I mean once in a while the day's pickings are slim, but food is abundant most days."

John nods in agreement.

I tell him about a hungry Sunday afternoon in downtown Asheville.

The French Broad Food Co-op was open, a few restaurants and Gatsby's bar. Vincent's Ear. All the other businesses were closed on Sunday. Town was deserted. Cold, cold winds whipped through the city canyons. I was freezing, hungry, and lonely. I didn't have one nickel in my pocket. For the first time in two years I questioned the sanity of living outside like a vagabond.

I was sitting on a bench beside the Vanderbilt Apartments, across from the library, where I was protected from the cold wind and in position to face the sun directly. Earlier that morning I'd picked up litter, hoping to find some coins lying on the ground as I have so many other times. No such luck. Nothing. Not a penny. I can check the dumpsters after dark, or wait for a better day tomorrow, I'd consoled myself.

A strong gust of wind swept down Haywood Street. I shielded my eyes from the swirling dust, and then turned my gaze towards the skies. I blinked and rubbed my eyes, certain I was hallucinating: I thought I saw dollar bills floating in the air! Maybe a dozen bills flying in the air above Haywood Street at the tops of the buildings.

"Oh, my God. It's impossible," I cried. Then, one of the bills shot straight to the ground. I was transfixed as I watched the bill dive towards the library and then fall to the ground on the lower level. The rest of the money was still flying high in the air, disappearing from my view.

I scrambled to the iron railing along the sidewalk at the main level of the library. The bill was lying in the grass on the lower level just as pretty as you please. I hurried down the sidewalk and picked it up.

Five dollars!!! I ain't lying to you, brother! What an impossible miracle. It was like a million dollars. I looked around to see if anyone had seen me. Not a soul, not even a car passing. For a minute I considered tracking the rest of the money down Haywood, but quickly accepted that I'd received my allotted portion and the rest would benefit someone else.

I walked straight to the Food Co-op and bought a sack of red lentils, a loaf of bread, and a chocolate bar. I returned to Badger Creek with my treasures, my confidence in living outdoors fully restored.

"Did I ever tell you about the first time I ate grasshoppers?"

"No, but I'm sure you're *going* to tell me." John kids me, but I bet he's never eaten one.

It was right after the Outer Banks walk, when I walked solo to Asheville on the Blue Ridge Parkway.

"By that point I'd covered over 400 miles. I'd ditched everything in my backpack except a mosquito net, a poncho, a water pot, and my toothbrush—and I even cut the handle off it. I had a little bag of coffee and some salt, but no food. All I had for shoes was a pair of flip-flops that I'd tied together with vines and padded with velvety mullein leaves.

"Anyway, I was up near Grandfather Mountain when I sneaked into a cornfield and ate raw roasting ears, fat with water. For two days all I'd eaten were violets, chickweed, wild onions, plantain, and dandelion leaves, so the corn was a hallowed feast for a lonesome stomach. As I gnawed on a corncob, grasshoppers landed on my hands and arms, so I snatched one and ate the whole thing in one gulp.

"The next few, I picked out bits of meat and tossed the shells. Can't say it was all that great, might have been better cooked, but the taste of any form of food is relative to one's degree of hunger. Later that night I baked a dozen juicy cobs in the fire ash. What a feast!"

John is laughing so loud I fear somebody in the neighborhood will hear him.

"What's so funny?"

"It's all Camper Dave's fault. He rolls into town and convinces all these people, including you and me, to leave jobs and homes and school and live in the woods. The other day I heard the owner at Beanstreets warning him to quit telling travel stories to her employees because some of them are ready to walk out the door.

"I know everything changed for me the first time I went on a walkabout with him."

"Hell yeah, everything changed. Thanks to Camper Dave, look where you are now," John cackles. "Sitting in a lean-to in the freezing cold, not a penny to your name, talking about eating grasshoppers!"

"Are you living this way by choice, John?" He stares into the campfire without responding.

"I always say I am, that I've chosen to live home-free, but in a deeper sense I know it isn't true," I confide to John.

"Just a few years ago I was bankrupt in every sense of the word. I was crazy as hell, strung out on alcohol, impossible to live with at home. When I finally collapsed to the floor of a mental hospital, I began to see more clearly how sick I'd been, and for a very long time. I was divorced from two wives and separated from three children. Surgery on my arthritic shoulder was unsuccessful. Many days I was incapacitated by chronic pain. Periods of mania and depression lasted months and grew increasingly more debilitating.

"I applied for and received disability compensation, uncontested. When the government's crazy-police saw my medical records, they signed me off as a certified basket case. All but about $100 a month from my disability check was automatically garnished for the mothers of my children."

John stirs. "I know you're crazy but I had no idea you're certified. You've got one up on a lot of us," he chuckles as he stokes the fire. Sparks fly as a cold gust of wind sweeps over the lean-to.

"Yeah, I'm certified, several times over. There's no telling what shape I'd be in if I hadn't met Camper Dave and walked away from everything. I knew I'd never be worth a damn to anybody if I didn't make radical changes. I'd destroyed too much. This way of living is far more than a lark or a strange way of dealing with a mid-life crisis. I was desperate for life."

I awake from an afternoon nap wondering if I snore when I sleep so soundly. I'm sure I do. I'm hidden in the brush thicket beside the Basilica of St. Lawrence in Asheville's central business district, with passersby all around me. When I camped behind a hedgerow at Sacred Heart Cathedral in downtown Richmond, my first inner-city camping venture, I woke myself in the middle of the night because I was laughing so loud during an absurd dream. Several times through the night I returned to the dream, sure my fits of laughter were going to blow my cover. Like now with snoring. I stuff my sleeping bag and poncho into my backpack and sneak out of the thicket, undetected.

I come to this place, or go to the Edible Garden behind City Hall, when the arthritis pain is too intense to carry on. I hide in the bushes like I'm sinking into a turtle shell, seal the lid and relax my nerves until I fall asleep. Usually, I awake and the pain has subsided. Today, good sleep worked its magic and I'm able to carry on picking up litter.

I walk deliberately with presence of mind, placing the trash in the garbage bag, bending over and stretching my legs, arms and back as I work. This morning I worked from about 5 a.m. until 8 a.m. Each day my goal is to clean five or six square blocks in the center of town before the people arrive to begin another day.

Most mornings I see Mary under the I-240 overpass, picking up bottles and cans. She's stooped with arthritis and holds up with a cane. We have nice talks about the good work of picking up litter as a form of meditation and an antidote to pain that's far cheaper than physical therapy appointments and traditional painkillers.

Plus we find all sorts of things, like clothes, tools, pens, caps and loose change, even twenty-dollar bills on lucky days; and we witness more action in the streets than we care to. Since conflicts between city police and the counterculture are increasing daily, I want to do my part to help diffuse the tension by cleaning the sidewalks and parks in the early hours and creating a peaceful presence for the new day. Like Mary does under the bridges.

I work my way down Haywood Street until I reach Pritchard Park. I pick up the few pieces of litter that have collected since I picked up this morning, then sit on a bench to drink my coffee. The daily patrons have gathered in the park, bundled under a hodgepodge of blankets and coats. Several people are wearing charcoal-colored fleece jackets, some of 150 donated to the Church of the Advocate a few Sundays ago at the afternoon free-meal for the homeless. Now, I see them all over town. I'm wearing mine underneath my overcoat. Team jackets for Urban Vermin, worn with great pride and considerable warmth.

The Asheville Police Department prison transfer truck pulls into the lane beside the park right in front of where I'm sitting, as it has every day for the past few months, ready to haul off drunks, prostitutes, panhandlers, hippies, and anyone else who doesn't fit the image of beautiful Asheville—the Paris of the South, as our city is touted. Our community patrolmen stuff their pants into jackboots, shave their heads, and tromp along the sidewalks like storm troopers. Five, six, or seven patrol cars, blue lights flashing, converge on one offender, and all this parade of power for nothing other than petty misdemeanors. The paddy wagon is necessary, one cop informed me, because many of the arrestees reek with foul odors and are too nasty to stuff into a squad car.

I'm reminded of a scene I witnessed when I was in Budapest, Hungary. I was sitting in Moszkva tér, a square on the Pest side of the Danube River. A throng of gypsies from Transylvania crowded the public space—some peddling their wares, some begging from passersby, some huddling together in animated conversation while sipping from bottles of homemade wine. Suddenly, perhaps prompted by some subtle warning I didn't hear, they hurriedly gathered all their belongings and disappeared into the shadows and crevices of the square. One minute they were there, the next they were gone. I was baffled. I couldn't imagine what was going on. Moments later, two police officers strolled through the area on their regular beat, crossing from one end of the square to the other. As soon as they'd passed out of sight, the gypsies reappeared as suddenly as they'd vanished, resuming the day's business as if nothing had ever happened.

Policing urban vermin in the streets of Asheville isn't much different. Even when the police catch people drinking or panhandling and issue citations or arrest them, they pick up right where they left off as soon as they're set free. I see it all the time. In street lingo, it's called "coming over the hill." As soon as they're released from the Buncombe County Detention Center, they walk over the hill to the center of town in search of the next drink or fix. Even when whole groups are aggressively swept away, in a matter of days a new group appears to take their place.

One morning I sat alone on a bench at the square in front of the Merrill Lynch building when a policeman approached me and ordered me to move along, claiming the chief didn't want anyone sitting in this area. Stunned, I explained that I'd been picking up litter and that I was sitting on a public bench, resting in the shade.

"The chief doesn't want anyone sitting in this area," he insisted. I didn't move, so he said, "You're just gonna cause trouble, aren't you?"

"Officer, let me remind you that all I'm doing is sitting on a public bench." He turned on his radio. Within three minutes of my refusal to leave, two squad cars—blue lights flashing—arrived on the scene, and three policemen threatened me with handcuffs and jail for refusing to move as I'd been ordered to do.

Fortunately, one of the officers took the time to inquire within the Merrill Lynch building as to whether the bench where I sat was on public land or private property.

"You're threatening me with arrest and you don't even know whether this is public or private property," I screamed. While I waited for my fate to be determined, the first officer who approached me said he'd heard I used to be a preacher. I couldn't imagine how he would know. With his finger wagging in my face, he demanded, "Don't you know God's Word says you're to obey the laws of the land?" I was flabbergasted by the absurdity.

When I'd first heard the term Clean Sweep Asheville, I'd assumed it was in reference to the Mayor's litter campaign—a thematic slogan to encourage the community to pick up trash on the streets and sidewalks. Asheville is filled with cans and bottles of every brand of soda and booze made in the last ten or fifteen years. Daily, the curbs are strewn with litter from block to block. All the city and county properties and parking areas are a mess.

So, I'd answered the mayor's call. I'd gathered my daughter Stephanie, Susie Mosher, and Snakehawke to help inaugurate the first mission. As we walked around downtown Susie fashioned a bouquet of wildflowers, Snakehawke blew his didgeridoo, while Stephanie and I picked up trash. Later I filled fifty-nine large garbage bags with trash underneath a bridge at the edge of city-center. I lost count of the bags I lifted behind City Hall and in the police-car parking lot.

Now I've made picking up litter my service to the community in order to pay for my right be in town, since I don't pay taxes, I'm not a homeowner, and I don't have a full-time job. As a litter-picker-upper, I'm on street level with a view of the rats in the gutters all the way to the upper echelons of the city's elite. I see firsthand the plight of the walking sick and the conflict they arouse within the community. However, one of the first things I learned at the onset of my new enterprise: Clean Sweep Asheville has nothing to do with litter.

When the police finally determined that all I was doing was sitting on a public bench, they left the scene of the crime saying, "We'll have to find something else on him."

That's when I first understood the true meaning of Clean Sweep Asheville. The trash is me and all the others sitting here in Pritchard Park wearing fleece jackets from the Church of the Advocate.

I cannot view the atrocities being perpetrated on some of the community's most defenseless citizens and remain silent. Without the help of many friends in my dark years, I would still be curled in the fetal position at Appalachian Hall—or be bones in a grave. The least I can do with my life is offer mercy for the poor and disabled. They are my family, as important to the community as the rest of the citizenry. Like me, many of them know the awfulness of a mental hospital, the abuses of fundamentalist religion, and the horror of mental and physical abuse.

A flock of pigeons swoop from their perches atop the old Woolworth building. I see their silhouettes on the sides of the buildings and hear the swooshing of wings as they descend to the sidewalk. They swarm around the bench where I'm sitting, bobbing and pecking for morsels of food.

One of the birds emerges from the flock and hobbles under the bench. I can see her through the slats in the bench seat.

She wobbles with an awkward limp, one leg shorter than the other, on feet like red high-heeled shoes, sporting a white nose ring and peering into the world with flaming orange eyes. She pecks at a piece of a cracker. Soon, her companions throng her, scrambling for a share of the goodies. With a burst of irritation she flaps her wings, fending them off, snapping at them with her beak. She only has to say it once. They scatter into the parking lot, and she nibbles her cracker in solitude.

She makes me laugh, not because she's deformed but because she's so tough. You have to be tough in Asheville, especially if you live in the margins. She, too, is labeled a pest, urban vermin with wings. Not long ago the city authorities let loose a falcon to harass the pigeons and clear them from the public thoroughfares.

"Hey baby, how bout sittin' on my face!" The man's voice pierces the noise of traffic and gurgling pigeons. The scene changes abruptly.

Three guys are walking into Pritchard Park toting a fresh supply of booze in a brown paper bag. There's no doubt they've been drunk for days. I've known all three of them for several years. Like so many of the alcoholics in town, they aren't as serious a threat as they appear to be. If fact when they're sober, they're good people. Today they're in rough shape. I'm sure the cops will arrive any minute.

Two kids on skateboards roll down the sidewalk in front of me. All the pigeons take flight with a rush of flapping wings, except the girl in red high-heeled shoes. She remains beneath the bench.

The men sit on a park bench, passing the wine bottle, leering and laughing at a young woman waiting at the bus stop across the street. I sit on the edge of my seat.

She's wearing a Phillies baseball cap turned backwards, long tie-dyed dress, an old bomber jacket, and tennis shoes with one red sock and one orange sock. She leans against a light pole at the bus stop and breathes a deep sigh, like she's weary tired of degenerate men making her life miserable. In her hand she holds a piece of green-cut bamboo fashioned into a flute. When she raises the flute to her lips, I see tears streaming down her cheeks. As one of the inebriated men staggers to his feet and crosses the street towards her, I rise from the bench to intervene.

As I wait for a car to pass, I hear little bells jingling. Snakehawke appears and heads towards the girl like he already knew trouble was brewing. He's barefoot with anklets of bells, sporting ragged short pants, a leather vest adorned with feathers and bones and a motley collection of I-don't-know-what. A tenpenny nail dangles from his pierced earlobe. He's tossing a lime-green softball in one hand and carrying his didgeridoo in the other. His blue eyes are set in a fire-browned face, like he'd just walked from a cavern deep in the Great Smoky Mountains.

As Snakehawke approaches the bus stop, he raises the didgeridoo to his mouth and aims the sound towards the drunken man, who is reeling across the street combing the hair out of his eyes like he's trying to look more presentable for the young girl. He stops dead in his tracks at the bizarre appearance of Snakehawke and his long aboriginal instrument, struggling mightily to comprehend his present circumstances. I'm sure he's never witnessed a more phantasmagoric scene in his worst delirium tremens.

Befuddled, he wobbles in his tracks in the middle of the road, staggers back to the bench, and gropes for the wine bottle.

"Whoa, ain't you boys a pretty sight!" Snakehawke raises his eyebrows and cups his hand to his ear like he's waiting for a response. The men don't respond. They look like three little boys caught with their hands in the cookie jar.

He closes his eyes and circles his hands in the air and breathes air deep into his lungs. He raises the didgeridoo to his lips and aims the sound towards the three men. The deep, otherworldly moan of the instrument confounds them. They cap the wine bottle, leave the bench, and disappear down the block without a backward glance.

Snakehawke waves to the girl as she boards the bus. He saunters away in the opposite direction, tossing his lime-green softball, chuckling to himself like his actions are all in the course of a day's work. I see him as a peacemaker, a community "policeman," an ambassador sent to bring goodwill to the streets of Asheville. I know him from the streets, but I have no idea where he came from, what circumstances in his life brought him to this place. He roams the streets all day in his crazy getup, on foot, bicycle, or unicycle, and is dearly beloved by all who know him.

Once, Snakehawke heard I was bedridden at a friend's house with severe pain in my arthritic shoulder.

He appeared in the bedroom with his didgeridoo in hand. Without a word he placed the opening of the horn on my shoulder and blew with all his breath. I don't have the words to explain how it sounded, but I could see the waves of breath and sound twirling within the muscle, bone, cartilage and blood of my shoulder joint.

The sound swirled in circles like the rushing clouds of a storm, suturing my wounds, medicating my pain, soothing my fractured nerves. I wanted him to play forever so that the pain would never return. Slowly, I drifted into a deep, painless sleep.

Another time he appeared at the door of a home atop Town Mountain where I was house-sitting. I was alone, beating myself up for being very insensitive to one of my good friends, bemoaning my apparent inability to have intimate relationships. I was remembering all the broken relations in my past and how I was the culprit in many of them. Suddenly, Snakehawke burst through the door without knocking, so excited he could barely contain himself enough to speak.

"I killed the scorekeeper!" His face was aglow like he'd come from the holy mountain with a fresh message for his people.

"What do you mean, you killed the scorekeeper?"

"I killed that little demon who stands over my shoulder wagging his finger at me all the time, telling me how sorry I am, pointing out all my mistakes and shortcomings."

"How did you kill him?"

"I blew him away with my didgeridoo."

I remain sitting on the bench at Pritchard Park, marveling at the scene that just transpired in front of me like a one-act play in the theater of the absurd. All the characters have exited the stage, including the pigeon with red high-heeled shoes. She'd slipped into the margins like a clandestine gypsy.

CHAPTER FIVE

Blizzard At Rattlesnake Lodge

As soon as I hear news of the impending snowstorm, I hoist my backpack and walk out the door of Beanstreets Coffeehouse. It's midmorning. I figure I can make the campsite at Rattlesnake Lodge before dark if I find a good stride. I'm very respectful of extreme weather in the wilderness, but not daunted. In the snowy cliffs just below the peak of Mt. Mitchell, solitude awaits me—a deep solitude, as essential to the health of my soul as water is to my body.

As I progress along Merrimon Avenue towards the outskirts of town I consider hopping on the city bus, thereby cutting my travel time in half. First I count the change I've found over the last few days while picking up litter—a collection of dirty nickels, dimes, and quarters, and a crisp one-dollar bill. Altogether, seven dollars and eighty-three cents. I quickly agree with myself that it's better not to spend seventy-five cents on the bus. I need every penny for beans and coffee in the cold, solitary days to come.

Already, massive black clouds are edging towards the northwest end of Asheville, blowing over from Tennessee, pouring drifts and drifts of snow into the Blue Ridge Mountains. The icy wind whisks littered paper across the streets. Despite the frigid air, I'm acclimated to the cold because I've been camping at Badger Creek all winter. I imagine the roaring fire I'll build at Rattlesnake. At the Badger Creek camp, firewood is scarce because it's so close to downtown, and we're constrained to burn low and smoke-free because the open fire is illegal *and* we're trespassing on private property.

While I mull over my outlaw status as a second-degree trespasser and illegal-campfire builder, an Asheville Police Department patrol car passes by me. The hairs on the back of my neck bristle. One day as I picked up litter around City Hall, I had walked into the police station and gone upstairs to talk to the chief of police. I knew the way because I've been to see him a number of times. I don't have a car or e-mail or stamps or a telephone, so when I'm inspired to speak to local government officials I go directly to their offices and request an appointment. The chief has always invited me right in, and we talk directly and to the point. By the time I leave his office, there's never any doubt where he stands on any given issue. I respect him for that.

This time he'd pulled up a chair and asked me what was on my mind. I asked him, "Why did you put 'Nuisance Abatement' on the side of some of the police cars? And who are the nuisances in this town?" He looked down at his desk and shook his head like he was thinking to himself, "Oh no, here we go again." Before he could respond, I suggested that some of the nuisances in town were police officers who break the law in the name of upholding the law, most specifically against those who are least able to defend themselves, and I asked him if he was comfortable with those kinds of cops arbitrarily deciding who is and who isn't a nuisance to be abated?

He resented my implication that his police officers were breaking the law. I told him, "In my estimation, at least 25 percent of the cops on the force are bad apples."

He conceded that some of his people don't execute their jobs perfectly. "Less than 8 percent are bad apples," he barked, "and we keep our eyes on them every day." I reminded him that I lived in the streets and observed the actions of the police from ground level every day. "Perhaps I have a better idea than you as to how your orders actually play out." He accused me of being self-righteous, and I said, "Maybe so, but the fact remains that the cops in the streets of downtown Asheville are nuisances in serious need of abatement."

I tighten the cinch on my backpack and get a move on. I reason with myself that after a week of wrangling with those sorts of things—the APD and Clean Sweep Asheville, City Council meetings, water issue debates, air pollution discussions—and hanging in the winter streets with the homeless, surviving a blizzard in the upper cliffs of the Appalachian Mountains will be a piece of cake. I don't know much about the game of politics, but I do know how to build a wilderness shelter in a snowstorm. I have a sleeping bag that could keep me warm in the frozen tundra of Canada, a rain poncho, and two tarps. Yes. Three days removed from powerbrokers falling all over themselves to grab a piece of the Asheville pie.

When I arrive at the junction of Merrimon Avenue and Beaverdam Road, I head straight for the dumpster beside Ingles grocery store to see what food is available before I spend my money inside. One night at a City Council meeting, I mentioned dumpster-diving in the context of serving free meals to the homeless and the enormous amount of wasted food in our nation. One councilwoman nearly gagged on her notepad. For most of my life, I would've gagged too. Now I'm just thankful to find something to eat.

The dumpster is about half full of garbage bags and boxes. The smell isn't too bad. I uncover a small bottle of olive oil to spread on the bread gifted to me out the backdoor of a bakery. Set behind the dumpster are two boxes of perfectly ripe bananas, not yet frozen. When I finish shopping, I'll grab a bunch to eat while I'm walking.

Inside the store I buy two bags of lentils, one onion, and a can of coffee. The cashier is amused when I spread my crude collection of road change on the counter and explain how I came by it. I stuff the groceries into my pack, pick up my bananas from the dumpster, and keep moving.

Negotiating Beaverdam Road is treacherous. Blind curves, no sidewalks, and scarce room for walking at the edge of the pavement. I pick up my pace, stepping around patches of mud and ice, keeping a wary eye for manic drivers on a mission to stock up on bread and milk before the storm hits. I inhale the scent of snow and laugh aloud. By nightfall the storm will bring the cars and the machines to a screeching halt. The noise and stench of this industrialized culture called modern will be cleansed from the air. Our ears and battered nervous systems will rest, if only for a few days.

I climb the dirt road, rising above the Beaverdam valley until I crest the ridge at Craven Gap. The extreme cold stuns me. Furious winds whip across the Black Mountains, staggering my footsteps. Icy flurries pepper my face and hang in my beard. Massive snow clouds shroud the mountains invisible. Hurriedly, I slip into the woods and access the Mountains-to-Sea Trail. The earthen path is stiff with rime ice. Thick icicles drape the boulders. I'm entering another domain, potently wild and alive. I sober to the moment and set myself for the final ascent to Rattlesnake Lodge.

Snowflakes burst from the sky, pouring into the forest like torrents of rain in a spring freshet. By the time I reach the grounds of Rattlesnake Lodge the trail is covered. I head straight to the crumbled remains of the stone grotto that houses the springs and drop my pack. The ground inside the grotto is slick with mounds of ice. Pristine water bubbles from the eye of the earth, undeterred by the freeze. I brace my legs to keep from slipping and stoop to cup the icy liqueur to my mouth. I fill my canteens and hustle up the hill to the camp. I don't have a minute to waste. Before dark I want to relax in my home and take off my sandals.

First, I search for raw materials to build a lean-to. I have pieces of string and two tarps in my backpack; otherwise, all the materials I need are on site. The mountainsides are a graveyard of fallen timber. I find a long, sturdy branch from a sycamore tree. The branch isn't perfectly straight, but it'll work. I lodge one end in the fork of the tree beside the fire pit. With the string, I tie the other end of the branch to the side of a sturdy sapling about five or six steps from the bigger tree.

Quickly, I gather six long branches that have fallen from the tulip poplars and break them into equal lengths. I set the ends atop the beam and then pitch them diagonally to the ground. I pull the larger tarp from my backpack, spread it across the frame of branches, and anchor it at the bottom with creek rocks. The opening is waist high. I brush the snow from the ground, pick up sticks and pebbles, spread out a poncho, and stow my pack in the dry.

Soot-smudged rocks are stacked high around the fire pit, which I rearrange at the opening of the lean-to, forming a half-circle about three feet high in order to deflect wind from the flames and radiate more heat into the hut. I tie the other tarp over the fire pit. The old tarp is full of small burn holes from flying sparks at previous camps; nevertheless, it will serve well enough to protect the fire from snow and wind.

I gather armloads of sticks and branches. I break larger limbs on the hard ground and snap the branches on my knee. I see several dead trees still standing that I'll save for later when the ground wood is buried under snow. Next, I strip pieces of hanging bark from the white birch tree standing at the edge of the trail near the springs. Birch bark takes fire even in soggy woods. Then, I snap an armful of dead briar stalks and place them in the dry. I'm ready.

I stand still in the snowy woods, pure white in dusk light. Icy clouds sweep across the cliffs and rush through the campsite. Arctic winds roar from the north side of the ridge. I'm taken aback by the fury of the storm. I hope the wilderness will welcome me and treat me as a friend. I feel secure, more secure than I often feel in town. I have running water nearby. Firewood aplenty. Sufficient food for three or four days, even some treats. My shelter is ready.

I'm still amazed at how swiftly these huts can be constructed and provide comfort in weather this extreme. Suddenly, wind surges through the camp. I guard my eyes from the stinging snow. Limbs from the trees snap like rifle shots. The tarps are ballooning like they want to fly away. I'm about to find out just how secure I really am.

With frozen hands and fingers (I don't have gloves), I manage to strike the match. Little flames shoot from the kindling and quickly gain momentum. Suddenly, the presence of fire enlivens my home and illumines the wintry evening a hundred feet around my campsite. I thaw my hands over the heat, chuckling to myself, giddy with excitement. I add more birch bark and sticks from the poplars and place larger pieces around the edge of the pit to dry. The fire requires diligent attention in order to maintain a constant heat and, in such small quarters, to keep the smoke to a minimum. I can't be lazy with the fire.

It's still early in the evening, maybe 8 o'clock, I don't know. I don't have a timepiece. The moon and stars are obscured. No matter. My eyes are heavy with sleep and my body is aching tired. I long for deep sleep—like the bears slumbering in the rocks nearby. Winter hibernation, a state of deep rest like the sleep of death. I stoke the coals and listen to the soothing voice of fire in the dark woods covered with snow. I curl in my mummy bag and sink into the depths.

Deep in the night the owls awaken me. Two of them, male and female calling to each other in the frigid night, their mysterious hoots from another world. One is perched in a tree near the springs. The other owl answers from the ridge above the camp. I toss more wood on the fire and blow the faithful embers back to life. I can hardly believe how warm and comfortable I am in my cocoon and how cold it is outside the lean-to.

I drift back to sleep listening to the owls. The profundity of their presence astonishes me.

A sound like a shotgun blast awakens me from an afternoon nap. At first I think I'm dreaming about cops firing guns in the streets of Asheville. Then, I hear a thud as a tree limb crashes to the ground near the hut. I scramble from my sleeping bag and crawl outside. The winds have awakened and are howling across the cliffs, contorting the trees in all directions, whipping snow showers from the frenzied limbs and branches. I spot the severed limb lying atop the snow, shattered twigs scattered across the ice-crust.

I return to my shelter and raise the fire—fully aware that my stick house provides little defense against falling limbs, much less entire trees whose trunks could crush me to pulp. The sheer fragility of life is before my eyes, as it always is, yet here in the woods it is acutely present and immediate. Slowly I acquiesce.

I stare into the fire and accept my death as imminent, whether here or at some other place and time, until I'm at peace. I remind myself that falling trees crush million-dollar homes and hurricanes sweep condos away like sandcastles at high tide. I bet the ice and wind have snapped power poles in half and power lines lay crisscrossed and twisted on the roads in town. Roofs sag beneath the heavy snow, and chances are there ain't one kilowatt of electricity running through the grid.

First light eases into my hut. I'm wide-eyed with wonder as the subtle glow illumines a winter wonderland. Surely the temps are sub-zero outside the haven of my warm sleeping bag. Over a foot of snow is piled up the side of the lean-to, and it's still falling from pure black skies. Shivering, I stir the ashes in the fire bed, uncovering the faithful embers that survived the long night. I build a small teepee of birch bark and briar sticks over the coals.

With a few puffs of breath, flames leap from the kindling, crackling and hissing like they're excited to serve another day. I return to the coziness of my sleeping bag and scoot close to the heat, my teeth about to chatter out of my mouth. When the fire is full, I retrieve a water bottle from my sleeping bag that I'd placed there in the night to keep from freezing, and I fill the pot. With a cup of coffee I bask in the heat and decide I'm well rested, like I'd slept all night in a soft bed, plush with pillows.

I sit perfectly still under my crude hut, mesmerized by the fire and the snowfall, listening to the whisper of a billion snow flakes lying gently to the ground. Otherwise, the wilderness is silent, the wind at rest. The limbs and branches of the trees are limp with snow and draped in icicles. I have no compulsion to formulate prayers or perform rituals or imagine gods and deities that separate me from the living presence of this moment. Only to sit quietly in intimate fellowship with that from which I'm made.

I've slept in the land of bears, coyotes, wildcats, rattlesnakes, copperheads, through rainstorms and flash floods, blizzards and falling trees, but not once have I been in serious danger. I've never been molested by the wilderness or the creatures of the wild.

Only humans.

After a lunch of cheese, flame-toasted wheat bread with olive oil, and a cup of sassafras tea, I entertain myself with daydreams about the night two Parkway rangers converged on this same camp and spoiled a damn good camping trip. To this day I remember every detail of that bizarre experience—a classic in the theater of the absurd. I was with Camper Dave, Flute John, and Mike.

We'd walked together at first, all talking at once, and then spread out to experience the wood's organic flow, each in our solitude. Unlike today, the air had been thick with humidity, as it had been in town all week, but dark clouds were gathering, pushing cool air through the dense trees. I'd found a sweet rhythm as I followed the meandering trail, lured by the promise of a sweet camp and endless stories around the fire.

But when we arrived, we found a NO CAMPING sign nailed to a tree, which the guys said hadn't been there in February. So Dave guided us to this spot further away from the trail and the springs. There was a wall of stones set around the oft-used fire pit, and a stack of wood lying beside it, like someone was expecting us. And there wasn't any NO CAMPING sign.

As darkness spread through the forest, we relaxed in our Eden, the light of the crackling fire glowing in our eyes. I was thrilled to share fellowship with these seasoned travelers, men on intimate terms with the natural world. We cooked good food and shared tales from our travels. The stories flew across the fire, our laughter ringing into the darkness.

"Keep your hands where we can see them! We are with the Park Service, and you people are in an illegal camping spot with an illegal fire. Stay away from your backpacks!" someone suddenly called out. Rangers, two of them, swooping down on us out of the dark, shining halogen flashlights in our eyes. At first we were too stunned to respond.

"We had no idea this was a no-camping spot. We'll be glad to put out our fire and move along," I stammered, trying to gather my senses.

"It's not quite as simple as that. You're on Parkway property, and there is no undesignated camping on Parkway property. You are responsible to know ahead of time where to camp. The border of the Pisgah National Forest is a few yards further up the hill," one ranger told us.

"Illegal camping in the forest? I just never would have thought of it. We saw the sign at the other site—that's why we chose this one. Why isn't there a sign here as well?"

"We put one up, but it's been tore down. We get a lot of rowdies out here drinking, causing trouble, and leaving their trash. So we've had to put a stop to camping right through here. Do any of you have firearms?"

"No, sir," we replied.

"Do you have alcohol?"

"No, sir."

"Drugs?"

"No, sir."

"We need to search your backpacks to make sure," one ranger said. Only moments before, we had been absorbed in tales of life and adventure—and now we were being searched like suspected criminals.

Dave and I rose to get our packs.

"One at a time, now," the ranger cautioned, blinding me with his light.

The closest thing we had to a weapon was one pocketknife among the four of us—that and Dave's bamboo flute. No alcohol. No firearms. No drugs.

"Don't you fellows even have a tent?" one of them asked.

"We carry one sometimes, but we didn't bring one on this trip," Flute John answered.

"Y'all sure do travel light. Looks like y'all know what you're doing—you're real outdoorsmen."

Once they'd determined that we didn't have anything illegal— since everyone was cooperative and amiable—I assumed they'd simply tell us to pay closer attention to where the designated camping spots are and bid us good night.

Instead, one of the officers said, "I want y'all to put out that fire and come on with us down to the car, so we can run a check on your IDs. You do all have IDs, don't you?"

"You can't mean it! You're not really going to make us walk down that trail in the middle of the night? You can plainly see we're not causing any trouble. We'll put out the fire and leave, first thing in the morning," I replied.

"You will come with us, so put out that fire and get your things together—one at a time," they demanded.

I poured water on the fire and scraped dirt over it. I broke down the bigger coals with a stick. I pulled the larger, burning sticks out and dug them into the dirt.

"That's good enough," said a ranger. "Let's go."

"I started the fire, and I'll leave it when I'm satisfied it's out. This bed of coals is still hotter than hell," I retorted.

"I can appreciate that," he stuttered, keeping his light on me. He could tell I was furious. I could tell they'd been watching way too much television. But they were intent on doing their job to the letter, and to argue would only make matters worse. Reason was out of the question.

"This is a sad day. This is really a sad day—illegal camping in the national forest," I whispered to the others. I kept muttering the words, trying to make sense of the concept.

So at 10:30 on a moonless night, we were marched single file down the mud-slickened trail towards the Parkway, one officer in front of us and one behind. My mind was racing as we stumbled along: How fucked up is our culture? Wrongful camping. Wrongful walking. Wrongful living. How far are we removed from any semblance of the natural way?

When we finally reached the road, we were told to get our IDs ready and to get anything else we might want from our packs. "Sit over there, away from your bags, while we run the checks," ordered the ranger, motioning with his flashlight. So we sat in a row, one officer shining a light on us while the other ran the check. By that time, I was too depressed to say anything—that is, until Mike politely asked if he could take a leak.

"No, sir. That would be another fine of fifty dollars for indecent exposure. When we leave, then you can sneak off in the bushes," the ranger responded.

"If I had fifty dollars, I'd piss right here in front of you." Dave grabbed my calf. He knew I was about to lose it. I sat down.

They checked us out, one a time, and we were all legit. They gave us each a fifty-dollar ticket for illegal camping, advising us not to appeal it because, "We're letting you off the hook on the illegal fire, which would be another fifty-dollar fine." The ranger went on to say that we could make payments—even if the authorities in Atlanta don't like it. "But if you don't pay, we'll do our best to track you down," he concluded.

I chuckle. I bet no cops will seek me out today!

I venture to the springs through driving snow to replenish my water supply. Sitting on a fallen tree trunk, I sip the medicinal water brewed and steeped within the dirt and rocky minerals of Appalachia. The water at Rattlesnake is a living being that seeps deep into my system, cleansing the toxins that twist my muscles into knots of stress.

When my shoulder aches like a dagger is thrust into the joint and nausea grips my stomach, I lie very still on my back, drinking water, breathing deeply, imagining the frosty air easing the tension of my enraged nerves. Pure medicine, curative and wholesome—far more effective than traditional treatments and drugs that left me bankrupt, remedied nothing, and placed a wicked scar across my shoulder.

When I see the scar in a mirror I'm reminded of the awful days, months, and years of intense pain I suppressed without complaint. I had to work; I had to function as a husband, father, and friend. I etched a mask of happiness on my face, when the pain begged me to groan and grimace. Then, bouts of pain followed by debilitating periods of depression. Now I know a way to treat my wounds and restore my inner balance. For one, I come to the winter air and spring water, purified by snow and ice, and make direct contact with that from which I'm made. I don't want a flashlight or cookstove or Therm-a-Rest or tent or books or paper or pen or anything else that hinders my intimacy with the natural world.

I watch the water bubbling from the eye of the earth, water so clearly sacred at the source.

It gushes from the very heart of these mountains, cascading down the slopes through an exquisite maze of tributaries like the blood of life that courses through our bodies' veins and arteries. Tiny rills and brooks converge, swelling into creeks and streams that rush through tunnels of laurel and rhododendron en route to the French Broad and Swannanoa rivers. Dancing waters leap from rock to rock, meandering through shadowy bends, swirling in granite pools, giving birth and sustenance to a world teeming with life.

When I turn on the spigot in a house and run water to take a shower or wash dishes, or when I uncap a plastic bottle, I'm little mindful of the source; conversely, in the woods where the need for water is immediate, I'm keenly aware that life hangs on every drop.

I fill my canteens and climb the hill towards the camp in the slippery snow. I gasp with emotion as I catch a view of the lively fire and my hut buried under snow like an igloo. A sanctuary in the woods. The perfect image elicits a longing from within me like whispers from the primal roots of my memory—a powerful, almost painful longing for a life lived with the earth instead of contrary to it.

By dusk, the blizzard at Rattlesnake Lodge has abated and only a few flurries drift through the air. The wind is calming. I sense that the worst of the storm has passed. I stoke the fire and make a pot of coffee and boil lentils with onions, garlic, jalapeno peppers, salt and pepper, and sop with a chunk of wheat bread. For dessert I eat half of a candy bar a friend had given me when I left Beanstreets Coffeehouse. I settle into my sleeping bag and see stars sparkling through the trees. I can't think of anywhere else I'd rather be than in this snowy camp at Rattlesnake Lodge. I'd survived the worst of the storm. It wasn't nearly as bad as I'd imagined, except that it's extremely cold.

It is already dawn when I awaken. No trees squashed my head into the ground and my blood didn't freeze within my veins. I build the fire and crawl outside the hut barefoot. I take a leak as the sun peers into Rattlesnake Lodge. The icy trees sparkle like diamonds in the slanted light. I scoop up a handful of snow and rub it on my face and clean my hands, streaking the snow with dirt and soot. In a state of wild hilarity, I trudge to the springs, knee-deep in a sea of white. When my toes are frozen, I rush back to the hut and stoke the fire until the flames begin melting the tarp.

Listen.

Thoreau, in a fit of ecstasy, is holding forth from deep within the wilderness: "Think of our life in nature,—daily to be shown matter, to come in contact with it,—rocks, trees, wind on our cheeks! the *solid* earth! the *actual* world! the *common sense*! *Contact*! *Contact*!"

I sit inside the hut drying my socks, thawing my feet and agreeing with myself that, all things considered, winter is my favorite season for camping. Not in town, but in the heart of the cold with a living breathing fire and the woods all to myself. In other seasons the bears and rattlers keep my senses at high alert and electrify the woods with their presence, and my encounters with them will remain etched in my memory. But I like better to enter their domain while they're fast asleep, so I can lower my alert system a notch or two and sleep free and easy.

I'm bonded from birth to dramatic and distinct seasons, seasons brewed and formed for millennia by the oldest mountains still living. I've walked miles of trails through the rain forests and cloud forests, from Rattlesnake Lodge to Shining Rock, Mt. Pisgah, and Devil's Courthouse in spring, summer, and fall. Fall, when the blood of the maples, sycamores, poplars, and hickory trees explodes through their leaves. Summer, among flowering rhododendron and laurel and 6,000 species of flora and fauna that thrive in the loamy dirt. In early spring, when the winds on Shining Rock twirl the campfire out of the pit, the flames flickering sideways.

Still, I love winter the best.

Especially for winter sleep in the heart of Pisgah mountain, arguably the most exquisite part of my life. I remember the words in the Bible ascribed to Paul the apostle, "I die daily"—a line I've meditated on for decades. I die daily when I fall asleep, most profoundly in the winter when the air is frigid to the bone and my sleeping bag is like a warm cocoon.

I imagine my death when I crawl into the sleeping bag and settle for the night. I take my time. I wait until I see my carcass entering the earth, my blood, bones, and guts, and see the bugs and animals in a feasting frenzy. I imagine a bear making my innards his own, or a mother hawk and her chirping babies feeding on my flesh and the mosquitoes swelling with the last of my blood. Often I awake with a start, surprised to open my eyes and realize I'm still alive. I die to the pain of tired, arthritic joints and the disquiet of my mind and soul when I'm anxious or depressed or too manic for my own good, and awaken with a renewed sense of balance.

And the very best argument for camping in the winter woods . . . the mosquitoes and flies remain dormant under the frozen earth. Hallelujah, baby! What a great relief. Through the years—with the aid of the invaluable mosquito net—I have adapted, but I don't miss their presence for a second. I've learned through many miserable experiences that they are the guardians of paradise who exact a toll for the right to dwell in their domain. They are worrisome still, but I've grown to respect that all living things have a distinct purpose.

My supply of firewood is running low, and the ground wood is buried. I take an hour or so to fell the dead trees still standing. I push them over with little effort, break them into pieces, and store them in the hut. I pull back the tarp that covers the pit and raise a bonfire.

I awake before daybreak. I have no clue what time it is. I can judge time by the position of the moon, but after three cloudy nights I've lost touch with the moon's location in relation to dawn. It doesn't matter. I've slept plenty. Sometimes in my camp at Badger Creek, I awake in the darkness certain dawn will spread across the skies at any minute. I dress, pack up my things, and head into town—only to discover that it's just 2 a.m.

I take down the tarp covering the pit and raise the fire to a blaze, heat a pot of water, strip naked, and bathe. I'm relieved to wash my long, thick beard. Three days of fire soot and food crumbs. I comb out the kinks and scratch my chin while I'm at it. Last night when I undressed for bed, I packed my shirt and pants in my pack with cedar sprigs. They're a little soiled and wrinkled yet freshly scented. I crush a handful of cedar needles and rub them into my beard and scalp for cologne so I'll be fresh and reasonably clean when I reach town. I don't want to smell like I've been camped in the woods for three days.

I laugh aloud. I'm all slicked up and ready to stroll into town, yet the sky is still filled with stars. Not even a hint of daybreak. I stoke the fire and content myself to wait for dawn. Maybe it's only 2 a.m.

The way of the trail is barely discernible in the snow cover. My sandals are wet and my feet are like ice, nevertheless I'm stoked for the jaunt into town along the gradual slope of the mountain ridges. I pay sharp attention to patches of ice and deep snow as I scamper at a pace just short of running. After three days of sitting still in the little hut, I'm more than ready for movement. At Craven Gap I take the old path that cuts across the west side of the mountain and merges with Town Mountain Road that leads into downtown.

The trees along the trail are posted with NO TRESPASSING signs, but I have permission from the owner of the property. I met the owner and his daughter when I hiked through one other time. They were riding horseback. I heard them approaching, so I slowed the pace and braced myself for potential trouble.

At first the man was obviously leery of me. I explained exactly what I was doing and pointed out that the trail through his land is the shortest distance to town, cutting in half my time on the paved road dodging cars. His demeanor softened as I talked. Then, his daughter recognized me from my photo in the local weekly paper for which I sometimes write commentaries about my view of life from the side of the road. I thought our situation might digress at that point, since my commentaries are often critical of the status quo in Asheville. He dismounted, shook my hand, and granted me permission to pass through his property.

It's only 10:10 a.m., according to the town clock near the courthouse. From the remote cliffs of the wilderness to the center of town in about four hours by foot! The wilderness is so close and accessible. The reality couldn't be more obvious. A new metaphor of faith, a turn of the prism, a revelation I'd never imagined. Walk out the door and take the next step and the next step, and a good way will open of its own accord. How could the obvious have obscured my way for so long?

At Malaprop's Bookstore/Café, I sweep the sidewalk in front of the store and set out their tables and chairs as I do every day I'm in town. I'm rewarded with a bottomless cup of coffee and a bag of day old bagels. In the café, everyone is talking about the storm and how no one has had a hot shower in three days. In many areas of town the power may not be restored until the end of the week. Two teenagers bitch about no phones, no computers, no televisions, and being stuck at home with their parents. Several of my friends are confounded that I camped through the blizzard at Rattlesnake by choice. I'm amused. From what I'm hearing, I fared better than all of them.

I head down to Badger Creek and build a fire to dry my sweaty shirt and warm my toes.

CHAPTER SIX

Summer Of The Children

Rays of brilliant orange streak above Lake Champlain, the reflections dancing like fire in the choppy waves. A flock of mallards shriek with elation as they sail into the Vermont sunset like they've just completed a long journey from Quebec down the Saint Lawrence River. Across the lake, shadows fold over the pines of the Adirondack Mountains, casting a deeper hue of green than I could imagine is possible. A swift breeze sweeps across the jetty where Stephanie and I perch atop our backpacks. We've just arrived in Burlington by foot, with this awe-inspiring wonderland spread before our eyes.

Joggers, strollers, and bikers stare as they pass by along the pathway beside the lakeshore. A gray-bearded man and a teenage girl with backpacks are hardly inconspicuous. Could they imagine that we're father and daughter and that we'd been walking for a week, over half the time in rain showers, and that we'd camped in the woods near the roadside? Or that we had come with very little money? That Stephanie had waited eight months to spend her summer vacation living the way Dad does?

As the sun dips below the horizon, I set my mind on securing a well-hidden campsite, very much a challenge so close to downtown Burlington and in unfamiliar terrain. I've honed my skills at finding camouflaged spots in business districts, neighborhoods, roadsides, and wilderness areas, places where I can disappear from the eyes of the public like I can at Badger Creek in Asheville. That camp is located at the bottom of a ravine near a four-lane street, only a few minutes from the center of town.

I explore the edges of a brushy, vine-twisted pine thicket on the other side of the railroad tracks until I detect a faint trail where the straw grass is slightly pressed to the ground. I wend my way into the heart of the thicket and discover a worn trail leading to a small area cleared of brush, evidently a former camper hideaway. I can hardly believe our good fortune, a home already prepared for us with no detectable signs of recent activity.

I kneel in the middle of the circle to closely observe the surroundings and make certain we'll be completely hidden. As always, I take time to envision a circle of fire around the camp to protect us from intruders—an even more important prayer ritual since I'm traveling with my young daughter.

I've stayed in the woods almost every night for the last nine months, so I'm well seasoned and in top physical condition. My senses are on red alert at all times, my vision as sharply attuned as the eyes of a hawk, and I have confidence in my intuitive sensitivity. To travel by foot and camp in the metropolitan areas of the United States in the twentieth century is always daunting because of aggressive police and hoodlums, like dealing with the threat of rattlesnakes and bears in the Blue Ridge Mountains. Nevertheless, I figure my daughter is safer with me in these circumstances than she would be in the volatile neighborhoods of Richmond, Virginia.

Stephanie and I have already traveled from the southern end of New Hampshire to Bellows Falls, Vermont, on the Connecticut River, and on to Cavendish and Rutland—arriving in Burlington on the Fourth of July. Each night we made camp in the woods off the roadsides, learning to string up mosquito nets and tarps while bugs pestered our hands and faces.

On rainy nights we pitched the tent, on clear nights we slept under the netting for a clear view of the night sky and a better eye for intruders. At the end of day two, Stephanie gleaned her pack to the barest minimum in the same manner as I did when I walked the Outer Banks with Dave. Motivated by sore shoulders and an aching back, she'd quickly learned the necessity of traveling light.

As soon as two joggers have passed from our view, I wave for Stephanie to follow me. She skips across the rocks of the jetty, hops across the railroad tracks, and follows me into the thicket. We string the netting in record time and scramble underneath to escape the swarms of mosquitoes that are rising in the twilight. I have to caution Stephanie to hold her voice down so as not to blow our cover. Her excitement is barely containable. Just as we drift into sleep we hear the night train rumbling towards us. The engine light floods our tent, and the ground beneath us vibrates like the train is about to run over the top of us. We laugh until our stomachs hurt.

In the mornings we pack our gear and walk to City Hall Park in the center of town. We quickly befriend a host of young people, many of whom are homeless and living in the woods like us, or surfing from couch to couch among a network of teens and twenty-somethings in similar circumstances. Stephanie, an avid gymnast since childhood, performs perfect cartwheels and standing backflips, wowing the kids and gaining us entrée into their circles.

As father and daughter spin their travel tales, our new friends stare in awe and envy, a desperate longing in their eyes for the family they'll probably never have. Every day I listen as they chronicle the tragic failures of my generation, particularly the fathers—most of whom seldom contact their offspring. Some have no idea who their fathers are. Stephanie and I openly share our own history of separation and loss, along with our food and water.

Prodded by the candor of the kids in the park, I reveal some of the causes of the irreconcilable problems between Stephanie's mother and me. Stephanie and I have stayed faithful to communicating since our separation, by way of phone calls, letters, and visits. I overhear her say to one of her new friends, "I've always been able to contact my Dad, even though he doesn't have a telephone and he's never sent an e-mail in his life. Sometimes it's kinda freaky. I focus on his image, ask him to call, and my phone rings!"

Our relationship is very strong and intimate; we've learned to cope, maybe because I've always spoken straightforwardly with her and she's learned to do the same. I taught her the fundamentals of gymnastics and the art of paying attention and, as a result, she learned to trust me. She is never hesitant to offer criticism that keeps my ego in check; she asks probing questions that challenge my honesty; and she reminds me that outside of the cave there are i's to dot and t's to cross.

I'd written her at length from Appalachian Hall; thus she's become very knowledgeable of arthritis and bipolar disorder and has remained eager to explore the causes and potential remedies, and she understands that my disease exacerbated many of our family's problems. However, I'd never admitted that I'd had an extramarital affair that had devastated her mother, a cruel blow to our struggling family. She'd heard the accusations for years, but had refused to believe her mother. She's clearly perturbed as I relive for her the sorriest times of my life.

Today we talked at length about *Demian* by Hermann Hesse, and the meaning of "listening to the teachings my blood whispers to me," a quote Stephanie's heard me refer to many times in letters. She's carrying the book in her backpack along with her journal, which she has faithfully kept since she was fourteen. I describe to her the many years I'd spent seeking the will of God and searching the scriptures for guidance, yet remaining in confusion and thinking that something was horribly wrong with me when I didn't get answers.

Everything in my religious experience had taught me that God is outside of us, not within us, and that Jesus Christ is the only hope of salvation from hell. For much of my life, I'd believed literally that our blood is corrupt because we are descendents of Adam and Eve, and that all humans inherited the curse of their transgression. My daughter's appalled that I could've swallowed such a preposterous notion. When I further explain that to trust my intuition or to listen to the whisperings of my blood was akin to blasphemy, she laughs at my ignorance. Her laughter is a great relief, an encouraging sign that she most likely will not follow in my path of delusion.

Stephanie vaguely remembers the Bible studies I had taken her to when we still lived together, but she had been too young to grasp what it was all about. Now, as she's beginning her own search for understanding, she's bubbling with questions about my religious experiences. So I share with her the story of the trip I'd made right before I met up with her, a story that well represents my religious experience.

I'd left Asheville walking on the Blue Ridge Parkway headed towards Virginia to visit an old friend from my early days as a preacher, who has built a worldwide ministry of evangelism and claims that many who come to his services get born again and that he heals the sick and casts out devil spirits. Recently, we'd had a chance encounter at the home of another friend in Raleigh, North Carolina, where he had regaled us with stories of the miracles he'd performed in India during a recent crusade. He had invited me to visit at his home in Virginia. Out of curiosity to know more details and from the promptings of my intuition, I accepted his invitation.

It was apparent from the beginning of our conversations that his mind was closed to considering anything other than what he believed God had revealed to him personally, namely that the traditional canon of Scriptures contains the literal truth of what God revealed to humankind for all eternity; that the second coming of Christ is imminent; that the earth as we know it will be destroyed in our lifetime; and that all Christians must contend with personal devil spirits. The same message I'd preached for many years.

As we talked, I wondered what Daniel was thinking—that I'm a devil; that I'd been led astray by devil spirits? I had referenced some of the Gnostic manuscripts from the Nag Hammadi collection that had been discovered in Egypt in the 1940s, many of which predated the manuscripts used in the traditional canon. I avowed that they added great perspective and historical context to the roots of Christianity. Also, I challenged him on the negative impacts of one-dimensional patriarchy throughout the history of Christianity, and the vital necessity of balance with the mother.

I was mildly surprised by his knowledge of extraneous gospels, revelations, prophecies, et al, not included in the King James canon. Nevertheless, he maintained the orthodox interpretation, basically saying that I was making a grave error by considering the extraneous works as equal in authenticity to the accepted canon. I told him I could imagine this same conversation between two people in the second or third century—the endless disputations, the accusations of heresy, the schisms between sincere people who purportedly had sought to follow the same Jesus.

When I suggested that we burn all the books including the Bible and the Gnostic Gospels and just live the life, he was as stunned as if I'd committed the unforgivable sin by even thinking such a blasphemous notion.

In exchange for Daniel's hospitality, I offered to paint the outside of his office, a one-room building beside his house. One day while working I heard him shouting, "Praise the Lord! Praise the Lord!" He called me into the study to show me the piles of money he'd collected at a recent revival service in Oregon. He didn't reveal the total amount of the offerings, but the packs of checks and cash filled a small suitcase. He boasted that one man donated his life's savings of $25,000 to his ministry at the end of a seminar on Armageddon and the end of times as it's written in the Book of Revelation. At that instant I knew he was incorrigible; few ever recover from crossing the spiritual line he had transgressed.

Later in the day I took a walk through the woods near his house, remembering the days when I'd preached the very same message until I was nearly 40 years old. With Daniel, I realized I was face-to-face with the dark, destructive side of fundamentalism, like I was looking starkly into my own life only a few short years ago. Then I spotted a solitary tree standing in an open meadow at the edge of the woods.

A flock of giant turkey vultures roosted among the dead limbs and branches. When the vultures detected my presence they took flight, circling the tree, and then soared over my head so closely I felt the breeze from their wing tips. I was stunned by the symbolism.

Later on that same trip, I met the sheetrock preacher.

After I left Daniel's place, I was en route to the home of another friend who also lived near the Parkway. At the end of the second day, after covering twenty-five miles on foot, I was ready to crawl into the woods, build a fire and make supper. I decided to explore the little ridge on the other side of the road in search of a good flat spot to spread out my sleeping bag.

As I was cinching my pack, an old dented and rusted Plymouth Duster pulled to a stop on the side of the road. The driver opened the door and started walking towards me like he had a purpose in mind, and yelled out, "You lookin' for a ride? I ain't going far down the road but I'll give you a lift a little ways."

Something about the man aroused my curiosity. Covered with sheetrock dust from head to toe, he looked like a ghost. His big belly poked out of the bottom of his T-shirt. I tossed my pack on top of his tools piled in the back seat of the Duster, and hopped in the car.

"Hope you'll pardon the way I look," he demurred. "I just finished a sheetrock job up the road there a piece and I'm on my way to the house. I gotta tell you, right before I seen you sittin' by the road I was praying and I ask the Lord what I could I do for Him since He'd give me a good job and I made real good money on it, and the Lord, he told me clear as day to help the next person I run into, so that's why I pulled over and asked you did you want a ride. You're the next person I run into." He was grinning from ear to ear, like he was proud as he could be of his good works.

"I'm an ordained preacher of the gospel," he continued. "Hope that don't offend you none?"

"No, I'm not offended. I appreciate the ride." I respected his sincerity and spontaneity, but I didn't want to get him started so I talked as little as was polite. I'd had my fill of religious fanatics.

"Yeah, the Lord calls on me to build up churches that's fell into neglect, both the building of the church and the people of the church. And I want to tell you right now, like I tell everybody, especially other preachers—I don't charge a penny for the work of the Lord whether or not I'm preachin' the Gospel or nailin' up two-by-fours. I don't quibble over it. I work with my hands and pay my own way. The church I pastor now offered me $500 a week to be their preacher, but I turned it down. If a preacher cain't pay his own way, then he's not the kind of preacher that Jesus talked about. Now, that's my opinion."

I wanted to hug him.

"I preach the love and compassion of Jesus to them that's buried in their sins," the sheetrock preacher continued. "I believe they's a devil's hell, but a lot of them that I pastor already know a gracious plenty about hell. What they need to know is that the Lord cares about them and that the Lord ain't standing over their heads shaking his finger in their faces."

I told him I appreciated what he was saying and that he's an exception to the rule. I gave him a thumbnail sketch of my conversations with Daniel when he was salivating over the money he'd collected at his revivals.

"Son, I tell you what I'm going to do. I'm going to take you to the front door of your friend's house."

"I don't mind sleeping in the woods. You're almost home and it's another hour to my friend's place."

"It don't matter. I've got all eternity."

"Amen, brother!"

When Stephanie calls to check in with her Mom, she informs Stephanie that she's putting Andy, my fifteen-year-old son, on a bus to Vermont because he's been very rebellious and she couldn't handle him. It isn't Andy's first choice for his summer vacation; nevertheless, I'm thrilled he'll be joining us. When I meet him at the bus station, he's somewhat dazed by the long, unexpected trip, but he arrives in surprisingly good spirits.

We stay at our home beside Lake Champlain a few more days to help Andy orient to living in the woods. Then we hitch a ride out of Burlington and make our way through the Northeast Kingdom of Vermont, across the White Mountains of New Hampshire, all the way to the coast of Maine with the intentions of hiring on to rake blueberries at the upcoming harvest.

Traveling by foot through Maine and camping in the woods each night, we explore Beals Island, Four Corners, Mathias and the barrens, where a purple haze hangs over the blueberry fields as far the eye can see, like the cornfields of Iowa. We eat berries until our hands and mouths stain with juice, and collect cans and bottles along the side of the road and haul them to the redemption center for a few bucks and some solid food.

We duck into the woods and make camp beside one of the hundreds of lakes that fill the north country. Recent reports of mountain lions in the vicinity keep me on red alert as we make a fire and cook our evening meal. As I'm reasoning in my mind that I'm less fidgety about encountering wild animals in the woods than I am of humans, I see the beam of a flashlight bouncing along the trail. I can't imagine that anyone could know of our camp. We don't have a car parked at the roadside, and I'd made certain that no cars were passing when we disappeared into the forest. I'd taken every precaution to camouflage our presence.

I grab a handful of rocks and demand that the intruder identify himself. With his badge in hand and his flashlight in my eyes, a local sheriff claims we're trespassing on private property and that the owner of the land is waiting for us at the roadside and that he's very perturbed that we're camping on his property. He orders us to pack our gear and follow him.

Stephanie and Andy had been in a deep sleep and are very disoriented and agitated as we gather our things and stumble through the dark woods. When we reach the road, I explain to the visibly irritated landowner that we'd meant no harm and that our choices for camping places are very limited in this area, and to walk on the narrow, winding road after dark would have been a dangerous risk to take.

His features soften as he learns our story. In fact, he hands me forty dollars, instructs the sheriff to give us a ride into the next town for a motel room, gets in his car, and drives away without further ado.

The sheriff is much friendlier once the owner has departed. He's amazed by the story of our family's journey and apologizes for having to uproot our camp. Not far down the highway, he pulls to a stop and shines his flashlight along the path of a dirt road. He says nobody would ever know the difference if we camp down the road a little ways and keep the forty dollars for food. We eagerly bounce out of the patrol car.

Late in the night, unable to sleep after the excitement of the raid on our camp, Andy and I have a long conversation similar to my discussion with Stephanie about the reasons for the divorce. I brace myself for his reaction, aware that he's far more confused about the past than his sister, yet he questions me like a sweet, fifteen-year-old son curious to understand the factors that had disrupted his life so abruptly. He asks me why I cheated on his mother.

"Because he's an asshole!"

We'd assumed Stephanie was asleep, so her infuriated shriek startles us. The string of expletives hurled my way, as a long-suppressed anger surfaces from deep within my daughter, catches me unaware. Waves of regret and sorrow sweep over me, staggering my senses. My inability to effectually cope with my illnesses and my irrational and immature behavior had caused serious harm to my kids. Her tirade continues until Andy is finally able to settle her down.

"Let her say all she wants, Andy. She has every reason to be furious. So do you."

Soon the three of us are wailing, tears streaming down our cheeks as the pain of our separation rips at our hearts. When Andy initiates a hug, our family experiences a moment of oneness that we'd missed for so long. Amazingly, it had taken a long walkabout through Maine to bring our deepest fears and sorrows to the surface.

Eventually our tears turn to laughter, and Stephanie shouts, "Do you realize we just got paid forty dollars for trespassing!"

Thousands of migrant workers throng into Four Corners, Maine, to work the blueberry harvest, arriving from all parts of the USA, Canada and Mexico. We even meet a family of Cherokee Indians from North Carolina who had just arrived from Hendersonville after working the apple harvest. We mingle with members of other indigenous tribes from upstate New York, Nova Scotia and Quebec, along with tattooed punks from the cities, teenagers on a lark, hobos, train hoppers, outlaws, and evangelical Christians. We walk the roads for two days seeking the proper places to register for work, and hop from field to field in search of a farmer willing to hire our team of three. When we finally have everything arranged, we find a camp spot for the night and wait for the word that the harvest is set to begin.

The next day as we head towards Four Corners for news of the harvest, a young guy from Quebec offers us a lift in his van. He's quite taken by our threesome of father, daughter, and son, and decides to seek work with the same farmer as us. We camp beside our designated field so we'll be ready to start raking berries as soon as the word is given. However, the next morning we hear that opening day has once again been postponed by the prospect of rain and may be delayed for up to a week.

"The heck with blueberries. Let's go to Quebec!" Vincent shouts.

Within minutes our gear is packed in the van, and we immediately head for the Canadian border for a week of camping in the Quebec outback.

We begin the long trek to Stephanie and Andy's home in Richmond, Virginia, hitchhiking. We'd traveled as a threesome for four weeks through the northern reaches of the states and into Quebec, and had only met with great kindness and overwhelming generosity and support. The kids are seasoned campers, toughened by miles of walking and camping in the rough. Awed by the eclectic people we'd met and the magnitude of the view from the side of the road, we head south towards home, buoyant, blessed as a family.

When I traveled with Dave, I'd begun to view my style of traveling as a school—the school of the traveler—with the journey itself serving as the teacher and classroom. With Stephanie and Andy as willing students, my vision has expanded. They'd learned the art of minimalism, how to not only get by with very little, but how to thrive. We'd carried only the basic essentials—a sleeping bag, poncho, tarp, water pot, cook pot, cup, spoon, and a few toiletries. With Stephanie for two months and Andy one, we'd spent less than $400.

Now, the kids know how to build a good campfire and how to keep the smoke to minimum for cooking, how to not give away our location where we had to be discreet, and how to string a mosquito net in the dark and stay content under adverse weather conditions. During many miles of walking and long evenings by the fire, we'd had ample opportunity for discussions on philosophy, religion, science, history, psychology, and literature. Our teachers were beggars and drunks, French Canadians, runaways, witches and preachers, Native Americans, world travelers, professors, politicians, and street kids.

In Connecticut we join a group of five other hitchhikers who are waiting for a ride on the entry ramp to the interstate. We'd been moving slowly most of the morning, with long waits and short rides. We wait for several hours with no luck, until a man in a pickup swerves to the side of the road and offers a ride to our whole group. Everyone hustles to gather their packs. My kids, filled with thoughts of home sweet home, a soft bed, a hot shower, and the certainty of Mom's food, await their turn to jump into the truck bed.

I'm the last one to reach the truck and as I do, a black veil drops over my mind's eye like a flag of warning. Not once on our entire trip had I assumed an adamant voice of authority in decision-making; however, this time I play my hunches and order the kids out of the truck. They're furious with me, yet can see in my eyes that the decision isn't up for discussion. Who knows if my intuition was signaling a warning or not, but only a few minutes later a very kind trucker in an 18-wheeler picks us up and carries us all the way into southern Pennsylvania.

The August sun is scorching hot, we have no food or money, and the kids are growing more and more irritable by the minute. We'd camped in a thicket beside the interstate, and we awoke with high expectations for good rides into Richmond before day's end. We manage to get a few short hops during the morning, but by midafternoon our prospects of reaching Virginia today are growing slimmer. Stephanie and Andy are at each other's throats, and my patience is wearing very thin. I can't believe that after such an incredible journey our good luck has run out. If I were traveling alone, I could stay content and wait, like fishing on a summer afternoon. But I'm not alone.

Finally, I walk to the edge of a field and specifically pray for a ride all the way to their mother's home in Richmond. The kids hear my profanity-laced conversation with my higher power and detect my frustration. With clinched fist raised in the air, I shout, "I want a ride to the kids' front door, and I want it right now!"

As I turn to face the oncoming traffic, an 18-wheeler hisses to a stop. For a few seconds I'm so incredulous, I'm frozen in my steps. The kids' jaws drop open. The driver opens the passenger door and motions for me to hop in. I point to Stephanie and Andy, to make sure he realizes I'm not alone. Overcome with shock, neither of them speaks a word as we climb into the cab—that is, until the driver states he's going all the way to the Virginia coast and will pass through Richmond.

"We'll get there some time in the wee hours of the morning," he surmises, looking us over like he can't quite decide what's up with the cargo he's just inherited. I'm so relieved I want to hug him.

While Andy and I sleep in the condo, Stephanie entertains Kenny with stories of our travels and takes a thorough course in the ways and means of an 18-wheeler. He drops his cargo in

Harrisonburg, treats us to an all-you-can-eat meal, and in the wee hours of the morning rolls his rig into the suburbs of Richmond, right to Stephanie and Andy's front door.

CHAPTER SEVEN

El Camino Real In Mexico

"Listen."

"What is it? I don't hear anything."

The crackling fire and the murmuring creek are the only sounds in the forest.

"I'm not sure. I thought I heard drumbeats, but maybe I'm just hearing things. I don't hear it now."

As Susie and I had walked along the roadside, we'd passed cave homes, crude stick-huts built into the sides of the boulders, and small log cabins. We'd spotted well-worn trails disappearing over the hills and into the pine forests. Perhaps drumbeats are echoing from a hidden settlement near our camp. We listen intently, spellbound by the sudden reminder that we'd crossed deep into the heart of the Raramuri homeland.

"I do hear something," Susie whispers. "It *is* drums!"

The woods take on an aura of mystery and intrigue, the drumming from another world and time. Again. High-pitched, tenor vibrations, the rapid beats twanging from the drum, followed by a series of echoes thumping through the hills. The sounds of the lone drummer continue intermittently until late in the night. We lie in our sleeping bags listening, expecting him to suddenly appear in the light of our fire. I imagine hearing footsteps crunching through the long-leaved-pine needles. I peer into the woods. The three-quarter moon illumines the trees and boulders with a startling radiance, yet I don't see anyone.

When Susie and I passed through Santa Fe, New Mexico, a friend familiar with the Copper Canyon had painted a romantic view of the Raramuri Indians in northern Mexico's Sierra Madre mountains where, he promised, our vision of a people still living as they did in the past millennium would come to life before our eyes. Cave and cliff dwellers who are world-renowned long-distance runners, they live in terrain so forbidding you can't imagine that anything but scorpions and tarantulas could possibly survive.

While in New Mexico, we hiked a trail through Bandelier National Monument Park at Frijoles Canyon—the former home of the Anasazi Indians. The faint hint of ancient spirits still roaming the mountainsides aroused my primal longings to live as they'd lived, the same way I'd felt when Susie and I walked through western North Carolina and eastern Tennessee, imagining the life of the Cherokee Indians.

And not with a maudlin romanticism. I've been living too close to primitive to be sentimental. All the rainstorms and snowstorms, mosquitoes, snakes, bears, and lonely days have cured me of any idyllic notions of a carefree life in the great outdoors. I long to understand the times before the white patriarchs with their manifest destiny stormed through the lands of the native peoples, before the onslaught of the age of technology and the gradual disappearance of the earth.

We had walked out of downtown Asheville with our backpacks, walked and hitchhiked to New Mexico, with our ultimate goal being Trujillo, Honduras. Neither Susie nor I had ever heard of the Raramuri Indians, but now there is no doubt in our minds that the Copper Canyon is our next destination.

The next day we arrive at a small Raramuri settlement near the highway, with a little store set in a tiny cabin. The stock is limited to candy, crackers, chips, canned sardines, and sodas. Two Raramuri girls with matching yellow scarves tied under their chins go silent when we enter. Unlike all the other women we'd passed, they engage our eyes. As we pay for our snacks, one of the girls thanks us in English. Her rich brown skin blushes red. We all crack up with laughter.

We rest on a bench on the porch and eat our snacks. Without explanation, Susie pulls a brown corduroy jacket from her pack and re-enters the store. I hear her and the two girls giggling like old friends. She returns to the porch minus her coat.

"Did you give them your jacket?" I'm incredulous.

"Yes, I did. It's the obvious thing to do.

"I still have my sweater and thermal underwear. Hopefully, the weather will only get warmer when we reach the west coast of Mexico, plus my pack is still too heavy. I have to lighten up. Besides, those two girls are so sweet and beautiful I had to give them a gift. I bought that jacket in my father's hometown in the Himalayas on a very cold day last winter.

"One night last fall in a field near my cabin in Madison County, I was wearing that jacket during a full moon eclipse. I danced on the hilltop and sang owl songs to the crazy moon and the starry night, when an owl at the edge of the field answered my hoots. Now, that coat from the Himalayas filled with full-moon owl songs will keep a Raramuri girl warm in the Sierra Madre."

By midday the sun is blistering. We take a break in the shade of a random cluster of boulders in the middle of a field. I'm almost asleep when I see a Raramuri couple walking towards us. They're as surprised to see Susie and me as we are to encounter them. The woman is carrying a baby strapped on her back with a fiery red blanket called a rebozo. She passes us without so much as a glance at the two gringos sprawled on the grass.

The man rides behind her on a burro, dressed in Western clothes except for huaraches. He slides from atop the burro and offers me his hand in greeting, smiling cheerily. Without a word spoken, he remounts his burro and follows after the woman. On the spur of the moment, I chase after the Raramuri man and offer him my coat. He shouts gracias three times, and then disappears over the rise.

Water drops sprinkling on my face awaken me.

"Susie, wake up. It's raining. We better pack our gear and build a fire. Pronto!" We stumble over the roots of the pine trees, still groggy with sleep and disoriented by the abrupt change in weather.

"It isn't raining . . . it's snowing!" Susie yelps.

I've been caught in storms so many times the drill is automatic. We stuff our packs, slip on ponchos, and search for kindling in the moonless night. A handful of pine needles crackle on the embers still hot from the evening fire. The temperature is dropping. Bleary-eyed from smoke and lack of sleep, we sit on our backpacks, huddled under our ponchos, looking for daybreak, constantly blowing life into the struggling fire. Regardless of the course the storm takes, we assure ourselves that we will be able to keep a fire burning for warmth and melt snow for drinking water.

"I can't believe we're sitting in a snowstorm with sunburned noses," Susie laughs.

"I know. We've walked for three days in short sleeves, throats parched for water!"

In the town of Creel we'd seen posters advertising Batopilas, a town hidden in the bottom of the Copper Canyon, where the weather is semitropical year round. We'd decided to make Batopilas our next destination, but now, trapped in a blizzard, it's difficult to imagine a place that's less than a day's drive where snow is unheard of and grapefruits are ripe for the picking.

When we walked through eastern Tennessee, we'd encountered heavy rains and had been forced to sleep under interstate bridges, and it had snowed on our camp at Badger Creek for several days before we left North Carolina, but I just hadn't considered a snowstorm or frigid temperatures in Mexico. I tell Susie the story of the camp I built during the blizzard at Rattlesnake Lodge, and how I'd thrived despite the conditions. I'm sure we'll adapt in these circumstances as well, I assure her.

As the pale light of dawn illumines the snowy forest, we venture to the road to assess our situation. The pavement is already covered with several inches of snow that is accumulating quickly. The boughs of the pines are sagging from the weight. The skies are black as night.

"The fork in the road, Susie!" My voice echoes through the vast silence.

"We know what to expect if we backtrack to the town of Creel. We know it's a three-day walk, but I bet we could catch a ride. We have no idea what to expect if we continue. We're at 7,000 feet or higher in the middle of January, so there's no telling how much it'll snow. Do we launch into the unknown or settle for certain warmth and security in Creel?"

I imagine the cozy little room we'd found in Creel behind Estella's Restaurant, the wood heater and piles of handwoven Raramuri quilts. Hot coffee and rich Mexican food.

"Let's go to Batopilas." Susie cinches her backpack and heads into the dark wilderness.

"Okay then, vamos!"

We walk into the pure, white stillness as deep as the sunken canyons on either side of the ridge. A subtle aura of great power emanates from the pristine woodlands. Rock outcroppings are shaded in ethereal hues of lime, black, mauve, gray, rust-red, and white, sculpted like chimneys and mushrooms and phalluses and giant dinosaur eggs. Two black vultures with four- or five-foot wingspans appear out of the low-lying clouds like a visitation from prehistory, their shrill caws as startling as the drums that had rocked our souls during the night.

I count my good fortune that I'd found such an experienced and enthusiastic traveling companion as Susie. To travel long distance by foot with a backpack and minimal gear is a new experience for her, yet her stories from the remotest parts of India and Sri Lanka confound even the most adventurous. She paints such a vivid portrait of Varanasi, I can smell dung burning and hear the drums and see her diving into the Ganges River. She's thirty years old and already a legend among the travelers of western North Carolina. In the streets of Asheville, she's an angel among the homeless and a creator of magical gifts.

When we first met in Asheville, we holed up in her cabin for the fall season, watching the leaves change color, reading passages of Rumi together on her front porch like it was our Bible—along with ee cummings, Zorba the Greek, Kazantzakis' autobiography, Walt Whitman, Thoreau, Buddha, and Jesus. Many evenings we read from the same dates in our journals. In 1987, Susie was sitting in Varanasi with the sadhus and I was in Florida preaching the gospel of Jesus.

Susie is very athletic, a former long-distance runner with the strength and endurance for a trek of this magnitude. She has no fear of nature, because there's no separation between her and nature. Like the Raramuri, she appears to have emerged from the soil, the stones, and the water.

I estimate we've walked over 600 miles since leaving Asheville, so our bodies are strong, yet daily we consider the value of each item in our backpacks, gradually discarding everything we deem unessential. I left a pair of boots on the side of the road not far from Asheville, content with the lightness of my sandals. We left some clothes near the border, and an extra cook pot. Our packs are much lighter, but in our exuberance to downsize we'd gifted our coats to Raramuri friends we'd met on the road when sweat was soaking our shirts in the scorching heat and the extra weight was tugging at our shoulders.

A two-ton logging truck with a light-blue cab appears around the bend. As the driver nears where we stand, he struggles to a stop on the snowy incline, gears grinding, the back end fishtailing on bald tires. The young man is as shocked to see two gringos with backpacks strolling along the highway in a blizzard as we are to see him plowing through the snow in a dilapidated truck. We'd never considered our circumstances dire; nonetheless, we're elated by his offer of a ride.

The windshield wiper on the driver's side is working; the other wiper, the heater, and the defrost don't work at all. The windows are open and snow swirls through the cab, the transmission groans and rattles around treacherous, hairpin turns—the tires only inches from the edge of the abyss. As I imagine the distinct possibility of the truck plunging over the side, I wonder if we'd be safer on foot.

A sudden break in the clouds unveils a massive gorge opening beside the road like a yawning giant, stirring butterflies in our guts. Brilliant sun rays split the clouds, creating twin rainbows that arch across the chasm against a backdrop of white snow and black clouds. We gasp in unison. The Sierra Madre, the Mother Land in all her glory, magical and mystical. Susie and I were born and bred in the Blue Ridge Mountains in the shadows of the great Appalachians, yet we'd never witnessed such magnificent mountain vistas.

In a matter of seconds the rainbow fades into rolling black fog.

Before he drops us off, Jorge, our driver, assures us that the town of Batopilas is not a figment of our imagination. The climate is semitropical with orange and guayaba trees bearing fruit, and only four hours away. "Seguro," he says.

Like two gringo icicles, we wait for a ride on the side of the road leading into the canyon while icy winds whip snowfall across the jagged mountaintops. The sun appears intermittently, adding to the surrealism of the setting. In a state of shock and awe, we wait until a guy wearing sunglasses, driving a new four-wheel-drive truck, skids to a halt in front of us.

We hesitate, unsure of his intentions.

He raises his hands in the air and shrugs his shoulders. "Do you want a ride, or not?" He speaks English!

"Where are you headed?"

"Batopilas, my friend, where else? Vamos!"

I motion for Susie to take the cab and I climb into the truck bed. The driver, named Camille—a gold miner from Quebec, Canada—tosses me a wool blanket. Shivering cold, wet and exhausted, we head for Batopilas and the promise of tropical weather! I'm elated by our great fortune, however I keep in mind that we ain't there yet. We still have to descend into the depths of the canyon, and the roads across the mountaintops are covered with snow and ice.

After an hour of racing through the sierra, defying the inclement conditions, Camille stops the truck and a Raramuri family climbs into the back. The man leans against the cab beside me while the woman and two teenage girls settle in front of us. We pass several clusters of houses in the desolate land of oaks, pines, and rocky fields of corn stubble. Two or three cabins together, stark and crude, a harsh world by any standards, yet the family gathered around me wearing colorful skirts, blouses, and knee socks show no sense of impoverishment. Their supple skin is lustrous in contrast to the gray winter light, and their full cheeks glow with their endearing smiles. The deep cold doesn't seem to affect them in the least.

We've walked a long way, I tell the man. He nods in agreement, pointing to our feet, side by side, clad in sandals with no socks, and our toes and heels mostly callus. I turn to face him. His deep-set eyes convey a depth of stillness like the full moon on a silent night.

As we round another sharp curve, Camille slows down to allow a truck to pass on the one-lane road. Thank God we're on the inside of the curve and not tightrope-walking the edge like the other truck. As we swerve out of the next bend, the long-lost sun appears in the gap between dark clouds like a spotlight, illuminating the Batopilas Canyon—so vast and deep it takes my breath away. Tears well into my eyes.

I struggle to comprehend the enormity of the precipitous cliffs. The impressive canyons we'd seen up to this point pale in comparison. Susie peers though the back window, her eyes wide with wonder and excitement. Even the times I've stood on the rim of the Grand Canyon, overcome with awe and wonder, don't compare to this moment as the Batopilas Canyon unfolds before our eyes.

When we reach the banks of the Batopilas River at the edge of town, the Raramuri family and I climb out of the truck bed. The man offers me his open hand and we lightly touch palms in the style of his people. We smile like old friends who've shared a sweet reunion. He stands as motionless as a stone, following our progress as we head towards town. I turn to wave again, but he has disappeared. I shake my head, wondering if I'd imagined the entire encounter.

Micah stretches his long runner's legs in front of him and slumps his lanky frame on the concrete bench as he tells the story of the three Raramuri runners he'd sponsored on a trip to his home state of Colorado to compete in the Leadville Trail 100, one of the most grueling 100-mile races in the world. The Raramuri placed first, second, and fifth. The winner was fifty-three years old, followed by his fifty-one-year-old companion. Micah carries the newspaper clippings to prove his tale.

Susie scribbles notes as he attempts to map a course of landmarks for us to follow to Urique, another spectacular canyon across the mountains from Batopilas: a bend in the river, a pile of rusted tractor parts, dry arroyos in side canyons, red mountains, white mountains, a ponderosa-pine clearing, a grapefruit orchard, and villages with names like Cerro Colorado, Yesca, Los Alisos, and La Laha. He warns us that the mountains are a maze of crisscrossing trails, and none of them are blazed.

"Do you have any idea how far it is to Urique?" I ask Micah.

He laughs with a mischievous glint in his eyes. "Anywhere from twenty-eight to fifty miles, depending on how many times you get lost. Once I got so lost I couldn't even figure out how to retrace my steps. Eventually, I ran across a farmer plowing a field in the middle of nowhere. I was too disoriented from dehydration to make sense of his Spanish, so I offered to pay him 100 pesos to take me by the hand and lead me to the trail. Another time I made it in seven hours."

"Seven hours?" I'm incredulous. "How is that even possible?"

"I'm a long-distance runner. I come down every winter from Boulder to train."

Micah abruptly rises to leave as he accepts that we aren't hiring a guide. He wishes us good luck and says he'll probably see us in Urique.

Several people in Creel had strongly admonished us to acquire a guide because of the bewildering maze of trails coursing through the canyons, the roughness of the terrain, unpredictable weather, and the threat of encountering narcotraficantes. Maybe we'll live to regret the decision, but we choose to rely on our own skills, as we've done from the beginning when we walked out of Asheville.

So far, we've traveled close to roads and towns and have had access to basic supplies. Now, we head into the mysteries of an unknown wilderness with no idea where we'll find food or water. Originally we'd planned to work our way through Mexico all the way to Honduras; however, there's no doubt in our minds that we've arrived at our destination. We want to explore the Copper Canyon and draw as close to the Raramuri as they will permit. Tomorrow morning we leave for a pueblo named Urique via El Camino Real. Plans for Honduras fade from our imaginations.

The trail winds along the Batopilas River, then veers into the Cerro Colorado Canyon. We follow the Cerro River through a shimmering landscape of cathedral-spired mountains jutting in and out of the canyon at random angles like sentient beings subtly moving in tandem with our steps. Thorn-studded cacti rise to the size of large trees. A flock of squawking parrots appear from the upper end of the canyon, frantically flapping their wings towards Batopilas. The sun illumines their incandescent green feathers. We count a dozen, but their squawks and echoes of squawks are like hundreds of birds.

Tiny hummingbirds swoosh close to our ears. Butterflies swarm the wildflowers, each splashed with unheard-of colors like in a hallucinogenic dreamscape, and the rocks framing them are banded in red, green, white, black, and copper. We pass under a sprawling mesquite tree abuzz with honeybees, like the tree is preparing to whirl to the top of the mountains.

Around another bend the red mountain comes into view, the Cerro Colorado, looming high above a cluster of adobe homes set at the foot.

We're greeted by a cacophony of living sounds as soon as we reach the edge of the little pueblo. The schoolhouse is stirring with activity. A woman is singing as she hangs clothes on a line tied between two trees; her adobe house with its turquoise front door is covered with the woody vines of bougainvillea. A lemon tree is fat with fruit. Pigs are rutting and squealing behind a ramshackle hut amid a flock of chickens, and a man is whistling inside. A second woman slings her laundry water into the dirt road near our feet. Embarrassed, she disappears into the shadows of her house.

Three Raramuri children follow us at a distance until we arrive at a shelter at the upper end of town. A beautiful altar is set with an image of the Virgin of Guadalupe, burning candles, and strands of plastic roses.

Our little companeros edge closer to the bench where we sit to rest before beginning the hike into the cliffs. Candle flame flickers in their eyes. I imagine that from birth, their full cheeks have been saturated with sunlight and moonlight, direct and unfiltered, in the hidden depths of a pristine world. Captivated by their glowing presence beside the exquisite altar to the diva of Mexico, I begin to question why the Raramuri are called primitive.

We follow their lead further upriver to the trailhead leading into the mountain peaks.

"Is this the trail to Urique," I question the little boy in Spanish.

"Si, senor," he whispers, his voice barely audible.

"Is it a long way from here to Urique?"

110

"Si, señor, es muy lejos." His words are soft yet confident, like he'd been over the mountains in his young life, or had heard the stories of his elders.

The children escort us 500 feet up the side of the mountain before turning back. Like surefooted goats they scamper down the rocky path, turning three times to wave and shout adios.

Dust swirls from our footsteps and sticks to the sweat streaming our calves and shins. The trail changes from soft, crushed stone and sand to jagged rocks that turn with our feet, then a level path hardpacked and smooth. Tight zigzags like a spiral staircase, and stretches of path two feet wide along sheer cliffs at the edge of the abyss—the margin for error grows very slim. Vultures glide above the trail like they're certain of our inevitable plunge into the deep. Our eyes stay riveted to every foothold.

Below us the red clay of Cerro Colorado is a mound of fire in the setting sun, the river a thin wave of streaming silver. The breadth and length and depth and height of the canyons are impossible to grasp. Susie and I break into laughter, pure emotional laughter like crying. We'd walked out of Asheville without a compass or a map and with limited money. We'd trudged hundreds of miles through rain and snow, blistering heat and biting cold, and have arrived at this unimagined moment and place in the Copper Canyon of Chihuahua, Mexico.

Gasping for breath in the thinning air, we reach a small plateau and rest on the cool side of the boulders. I figure we have three hours before dark and at least 1,000 feet to climb before we reach the top. Hopefully, we'll reach the ponderosa clearing Micah had described and find a flat area to sleep for the night. I take note of black clouds floating over the sierra as we rise above the land of cacti and mesquite and enter a bioregion of dwarf oak and pine, decorated with sprawling plants of aloe and flowers painted yellow and faint blue.

We reach the base of the rocky spires as the tip of the sun sits atop the distant peaks, casting an otherworldly light into the depths of the cavern, the last rays like streaks of fire over the vast ranges of jagged stone.

Early the next morning we follow a smooth, level trail beneath a canopy of long-needled pines giving way here and there to views of the great, stone chimneys directly above us—and to the other side, glimpses of the great void that take our breath. After a couple of hours, the path abruptly veers downward, winding into the bottom of a deep arroyo strewn with boulders, and then the trail vanishes. For an hour or more we search for a way through the creek bed. We retrace our steps again and again until we're totally baffled. Once again, fighting disorientation, Susie winds through the boulders and picks up the trial on the other side of the embankment.

We drop our packs, share peanuts, and settle our nerves. What a relief to find the way; how disconcerting to lose it.

In the afternoon the sun begins to disappear behind increasing clouds, some of which are splayed at their edges like wild, spectral beings. Robust surges of wind swirl dust in the trail and zip leaves through the air. Susie and I are silent, only staring at our feet and the next step, remembering snowstorms and rainstorms. Then the clouds break, and sunlight sweeps across the path creating an ambience of mystery and overwhelming power, leaving us lightheaded and increasingly unsettled.

And the pathway grows more illusive, in and out of arroyos, leveling for a long stretch, then gradually becoming fainter and fainter. In some places the trail is covered with fallen leaves. We scan the ground searching for footprints and animal droppings, growing doubtful of our direction, remembering the words of Micah when I asked him how far it is to Urique, "Depends on how many times you get lost." And the admonitions of the men in Creel, "Get a guide. Get a guide. The mazes of trails through the sierra are nearly impossible to follow."

The temperature continues to drop. A mist of rain sweeps across the mountains. Another split in the trail. We choose the one that follows a small creek bed as the rain turns to snow and sleet, changing to rain, and then snow and sleet until the trail disappears. Icy surges of wind sting our eyes. As we pass through a field of corn stubble, a hawk appears from the fog, glides along the top of the ground, then soars back into the fog out of our sight. Are we hallucinating? Is the lightness of air at these altitudes conspiring with our adrenalin to play tricks on us? Is the eerie wind intent on further confusing two lost gringos?

When we left Batopilas, I was confident we'd find our way to Urique without any problems. I'd spent most of my life hiking through the mountain ranges of western North Carolina, never fearing for a moment that I'd get lost. But now, face-to-face with the raging elements of the Sierra Madre, we are utterly lost and aware that the Mother Mountains have no regard for our plight.

Susie clasps my arm and points ahead.

Through the snow shower we sight a small thatched hut with smoke swirling from a tin-can chimney. One side of the hut is open to the weather. We veer from the creek side and edge along the rise, hardly believing our eyes. A tiny Raramuri woman is sitting in a wooden chair by a small fire. We move within her view, keeping a respectful distance, waiting for her to acknowledge our presence.

"Con permiso?" I call for permission to approach her, but she doesn't flinch. Two white foreigners have appeared from the storm clouds with backpacks and ponchos, and she's not reacting to us.

Are the howls of the wind muffling our footsteps and our whispers?

I step closer.

Her yellow and green shawl reflects the fire and her deep-set Raramuri eyes. She's shelling corn onto the lap of her apron. I scan the grounds for signs of others. The woman is alone, I surmise, and away in a reverie, cozy with her fire in a hut atop the world. Maybe she's blind or deaf, but I really don't think so. She's just ignoring us.

"We've entered another dimension, Susie. She doesn't even see us. We're invisible." I hold Susie's arm and attempt to joke, but in the surreal circumstances the possibility of our invisibility is too real.

"Mickey, let's go. Come on."

The woman continues shelling corn, unperturbed by the wild weather or alien backpackers.

We drift along the side of the hill in a daze, confused and very dejected that the woman hadn't responded. Our hopes had soared at the prospect of refuge, or at the least directions to the trail to Urique. I'm convinced we're close to the edge of the Urique Canyon, I tell Susie. If we could just find the trail, we could possibly make the descent into warmer weather. If not, we need to make a shelter—soon—and build a fire to ward off frostbite.

Then, we come to another hut, larger than the other home and closed on all sides. A young Raramuri girl wearing a red, short-sleeved dress is standing in the doorframe, smiling. She's barefoot and grinning like she's amused by our sudden appearance. A small, bony dog is yelping at the side of the house. The girl shoos him away with a clap of her hands.

"Con permiso?"

"Si, pasale," she responds with a quiet, gentle voice, seemingly undaunted by our sudden appearance and fully aware of our predicament.

As we tentatively approach the house, Susie and the Raramuri girl stare in wonder at each other—and then burst into laughter. All three of us dissolve into an inexplicable state of hilarity. I can't believe what I'm witnessing. Not ten minutes ago I was preparing myself for the worst. The elder woman had shunned us, or we had scared her out of her wits. With this girl we're like old friends. She holds her hands to her mouth to stifle her laughter. It's no use. She's cracking up.

Her name is Julia, seventeen years old. When I try to explain that we're lost, she breaks down while Susie cackles along with her. I'm sure the silent woman at the other hut hears everything and decides we're insane creatures from another existence and that she'd made a good decision to ignore us.

Julia graciously fills our water bottles and points to a shed near the house.

"Espere te! Espere te aya!

She watches from her front door until we're situated inside the shed, her eyes shiny with excitement.

A downpour of rain mixed with sleet pelts the tin roof. Every surge of wind lifts sheets of tin from the beams, clattering and creaking, and sprays snow through the opening between the walls and the roof. We settle close to the wall, the only dry spot in the shed, and huddle under our ponchos for warmth. It's all we need. Cramped into a sliver of dry earth, we couldn't be more ecstatic if we'd found the treasure of the Sierra Madre. Then again, maybe we did. Lost in a blizzard, we'd found a home among the Raramuri.

We sit for a couple of hours, growing weary as the traces of daylight begin to fade. Only a few flurries of snow drift in the air, but the eerie wind still roars across the tops of the cliffs. We drift between dream-filled sleep and wakefulness, no longer sure of the difference.

Footsteps crunch through the ice near the shed. I wipe the grogginess from my eyes and struggle to my feet. An older Raramuri man wearing huaraches with no socks, black jeans, a white shirt buttoned to the collar, and a Dallas Cowboy jacket appears at the door. He eyes us like he's assessing the circumstances and considering what to do with two lost gringos abruptly thrown into his lap. No words and no change in his demeanor.

He steps inside and I offer my hand in greeting, remembering to leave my hand open and only brush palms. He returns my greeting and motions for us to follow. We make our way across the meadow, retracing our steps from only a few hours ago when time stood still, the odds stacked against us. My only thought is that timing is everything.

We pass the three-sided hut of the silent woman. Inside, a crude, stick-wood bed is covered with blankets and a few cook pots hang from the posts of the hut. Hay is stacked in the corner and a fire pit with four rocks is set on the ground at the opening. A stone metate for grinding corn leans against an old, worn tree stump. A few odds and ends and nothing more. There's no sign of the woman.

The man leads us to another hut that we hadn't even seen earlier. He opens the lock with a key and starts kicking old pieces of wood and shards of clay pots to the edge of the dirt floor and attempts to close the wooden shutters on the only window, but the wind blows them open. Yet to speak a word, he leaves the hut and walks up the hill behind the house.

As we attempt to scrape together kindling, our host returns with an armload of wood. We kneel together and light the fire. When he's satisfied that we're comfortably situated, he leaves without a word.

"Home sweet home, Susie."

Early the next morning I venture outside for more firewood. Light snow is still falling. The cold bites my face. The snow-covered field is shrouded in thick fog. I recall the view of the mountains from the Cerro Colorado River and how I couldn't have imagined a trail through the peaks, or that any one could possibly live there. And how Micah had described the strength of the Raramuri people, their superhuman stamina for running. How hardy a soul must come from these parts, living with almost nothing in the aeries of the Copper Canyons, a thousand years removed from the twentieth century.

We make coffee and snuggle into our sleeping bags, reconciling ourselves to the fact that we'll be sitting in the cabin for at least another day and night. Inside the little hut, there is little difference between day and night. We sit in a surreal world of smoke, fire, dirt, and freezing air. The silence is palpable. We hear the long, hoarse bellow of a burro. Deep in the night, the braying sounds like the screams of a baby, carried by the howling wind.

As we sit in the profound isolation, I evaluate my investments of time and energy in the path of minimalism—that less is more— and if it had and would continue to pay valuable dividends for my family and for the families in the community where I live. I share my thoughts with Susie, and she coaxes me to allow myself sufficient time to heal and gain great strength so that I never return to the vicious cycles of mania and depression. We concur that the spa of the wilderness has been a far more rational choice for health care than mental hospitals and welfare.

Lying still beside the fire, listening to the sounds of the wind howling as it has since the beginning of time, I absorb the elemental power within my being. In the lonely, snow-swept mountains, I commune with the creative light that flows through all things. For now, no printed word to contemplate, nobody's

opinions or interpretations to consider, no theories to explore—
only direct contact with the air and the earth, the moon and the
snow, receiving the Logos straight from the source, free of filter,
like the canyon moon, brilliant and undiluted.

I thought we'd lost our way across the mountaintops, perhaps
fatally so; that I'd overstepped the boundaries of fate, and that
our final moments of this life would expire in the frozen tundra
of a faraway land. I wrap tight in my sleeping bag, now safe and
secure within the holy of holies.

At daybreak on the third morning, the man knocks on our door
and announces that he will now lead us to the trail to Urique. We
pack our gear and follow him through the meadow, giddy with
excitement. We climb over a stone wall that separates two fields
of corn stubble, and then head towards a rock escarpment. We
hear what sounds like animated laughter. As we draw closer to the
cave-like recess, we espy five men sitting by a fire. Five mules and
four burros are tied under the rock. Gear is stacked behind them,
along with a dozen or more large feed sacks. Our guide leads us
into the makeshift camp.

The men welcome us into their circle around the fire and
offer a drink from their bottle of tequila. Obviously friends of our
guide, it appears they had camped through the storm same as us.
When Susie takes a swig of tequila without flinching, the men are
impressed. They're a jovial bunch, like they'd had a good supply
of tequila for the entire three-day layover.

Two of the men appear to be mestizos, the three younger
guys are Raramuri. All are armed with pistols and knives and two
have bandoliers stretched across their chests. The guardian of the
tequila bottle is minus two front teeth and wears a patchy beard
and a red scarf tied around his neck.

I ask him why he didn't bring tequila over to our hut during
the storm. He laughs and makes a joke to the delight of all his
buddies, but we don't understand a word he's saying. He retrieves

a bean burrito from the fire ash and offers it to Susie and me. We'd eaten very little during our confinement, so we readily accept. What could be more appropriate under the circumstances than burritos and tequila for breakfast with a band of old-style Mexican cowboys.

Susie tilts her head back, sniffing the air while looking at our guide. He smiles for the first time since we'd met and holds his fingers to his lips like he's smoking a cigarette. I catch the scent. The dozen or so feedbags stacked in the back of the cave are filled with marijuana.

The man with two missing teeth drags one of the bags from the stack, unties the top, and offers me a handful of weed. He insists that I smoke. I beg off, explaining that I don't want to walk down the mountains on an icy trail high on marijuana. Thankfully, he's satisfied. We'd heard the rumors about violent narcotraficantes. Several people in Creel had warned that the drug traffickers in the canyons are very dangerous. Maybe so, but these guys couldn't be friendlier or more hospitable.

We remain by the campfire while the men prepare to leave. They tie the sacks of marijuana onto the backs of the burros and saddle their horses. They shake our hands and wish us good luck, and claim that Urique is only a few hours down the trail. They mount their rearing horses and gallop across the meadow, shouting and firing their pistols into the air.

Our guide leads us to the edge of the meadow and points to the trail less than a ten-minute hike from the cave. So close to the trail the whole time! We weren't lost at all. After three days suspended in time and place, we're ecstatic to be on our way, like we're heading home after a long, difficult absence. Our guide says the trail is very clear all the way to Urique. We gift him some pesos since we have nothing else to offer. He walks away without responding.

As we begin our descent, Susie clutches my arm and says the silent Raramuri woman had looked her in the eyes with a slight smile as we walked away from their hut.

We descend the mountain peaks at a snail's pace. Giant icicles hang from the boulders, and in the shaded recesses of the cliffs the narrow, rock-based trail is covered with ice. Without ice, the descent would be treacherous; one misstep, and we slide into oblivion. One measured step at a time, testing the path for traction, we inch along the ledges with a view of the pencil-thin Urique River winding through the bottom of the vast canyon far, far below.

As we descend, the air grows warmer and warmer, like we're slowly emerging from the ice age and entering a giant sauna where spring and winter intermingle. Inspired by the promise of relief from the bitter cold and a path free of ice, we wind our way through a long series of switchbacks, then a stretch that's almost a vertical descent with little on the trail for traction. Down another winding staircase until we merge onto a smooth, level path where a massive boulder juts over the edge of the inner canyon. We can see the white caps in the shoals of the river, and large emerald pools, and the way of the trail running at a gradual descent along the side of the mountain. Almost home!!

Ya meiro!

As soon as we reach the sandy beach beside the Urique River, we fall to our knees and kiss the sand. Susie changes into short pants and we dive into the pool. Our deep sighs of relief echo in the narrow canyon. We stand together staring at the massive, snowcapped peaks like we're trying to remember the details of a dream.

Suddenly, not in the least daunted by our presence, a hawk nosedives towards the river and snatches a fish from the shallows below the pool. He flaps his wings through the canyons, clutching his prize still dripping with water. I shout a salute. The echo of my voice accompanies the hawk until it disappears around the next bend down river. The sight of the fantastic bird coaxes us onward, a sign that the unknown path ahead of us is a treasure land of wondrous sights and experiences.

Just before dark, after seven more miles of walking on a dirt road that skirts the edge of the river, we enter Plaza Restaurant in downtown Urique. We sit on the patio in a tropical garden, eating beans and tortillas and drinking beer until late in the evening. We'd survived the winter storm. Sheer relief keeps us from collapsing with exhaustion. Later we'll search for a spot on the river and camp for the night. In the morning we'll figure out where the hell we are.

CHAPTER EIGHT

You Can't Go Home Again

I settle into a couch at Beanstreets Coffeehouse and sip a cup of hot tea—about sixteen hours since Susie and I arrived from Semana Santa in the Copper Canyons. After four months of sitting on rocks, the soft seat and the commingling aromas of scones and bagels and the chatter of early morning patrons lull me into a sleepy reverie. I see two red-breasted trogons feeding on tiny mango buds at our camp in Urique, dropping juice on our arms like sprinkles of rain. I watch them playing in the giant palo alto tree, flitting from branch to branch, eating, singing, and making love.

The noisy magpie jays appear, three or four times larger than the blue jays of western North Carolina, cruising the arroyo, singing and whistling in four or five distinct tongues, eight or ten of them darting across the treetops like a band of rowdy gypsies. They are adorned with long, plumed tails and an unkempt tuft of hair like an Indian headdress, their wild eyes peering from within an ancient world.

Raramuri drumbeats still ring my ears. The sand of the Urique River is in my clothes, my hair and behind my ears. I'm saturated with incense of achiote and pinewood bonfires. Painted Raramuri dance through my mindscape in a cloud of dust.

Tim rushes through the door of the coffeehouse and plops beside me on the sofa, snapping me out of dream world. He clutches my arm and demands that I follow him outside. He insists that there's trouble brewing at the square. I don't want to go with him. I'm settled in at base camp like a purring cat. Besides, Tim has done this before—I'll hurry down the street with him like we're going to put out a fire, and he forgets where he's going before we ever get there.

He grips my arm until it hurts. He's relentless. I have to go. He leads me over the hill to the square to the front of the Pack Place building and points to a group of people eating at a free meal. Some of my friends are serving the food. Beside the table, another friend is in a heated discussion with a police officer.

My friend is explaining to the policeman that she doesn't think it's necessary to have a permit to serve free food to the homeless, since the meal has been ongoing for two months with the permission of the management at Pack Place. She points out that police officers have passed by many times without saying anything. And look how peaceful it is, she pleads.

The cop remains calm, listening to the pleas of the young woman. Nonetheless, he is not wavering from his intention to close down the operation. "We've had complaints from some of the downtown merchants, and it's my job to protect our customer base," he avows. "You will have to go to the Parks and Recreation Department at City Hall and apply for a permit. That's how the ordinance reads, and that's all there is to say about it. Now, y'all need to clean up your things and move along."

"We're here to protect our customer base." How many times have I heard that claim, and he's so cavalier about it, like there's no question that's the responsibility of the APD. I want to throw his gun in the bushes and wrestle him to the ground so he understands once and for all that the municipal police are not corporate militia and the people of the Asheville community are not under martial law. If he has decided he's closing down the meal, then there ain't a damn thing we can do about it. But don't say you're here to protect your customer base.

Then I notice he's wearing a WWJD wristband. "What would Jesus do?" So I interject myself into the conversation.

"Wouldn't it have been funny if Jesus had been required to run and get a permit before he fed the 5,000 with loaves and fishes?" I point to his wristband and raise my arms in the air to invite his answer, and laugh to indicate to the police officer that I think it would be funny.

I turn to leave before I get into serious trouble. I want to return to the sofa at Beanstreets and visit with my friends. Later, I plan to get some sleep at Badger Creek.

"Yeah, but Jesus isn't here!" The officer barks his reply like a riled-up dog. I stop in my tracks.

"Well, if Jesus *was* here, he'd probably kick your ass," I retort.

I walk in handcuffs with the young police officer to the Buncombe County Detention Center, three blocks away. Tim is at my side. He's confused and very perplexed as to why I'm in handcuffs. I assure him that I'm okay. Most of the people from the free meal are following as well. One girl is arguing with the cop to take off the cuffs and let us all go home, no harm done. No response. He's nervous. I'm sure he's trying to figure out what charge to pin on me when we reach the jailhouse. Plus, Tim is glaring at him, and Tim is very big and strong and more than a little crazy. I figure I may as well forget the comfortable sofa at Beanstreets.

I hear the door slam shut at the entrance. Another "criminal" incarcerated, I imagine.

"We've got us a female, boys," shouts the jailer. He's sitting on the other side of the room where he has a view of the entrance.

"Is it any good?" laughs one of the city cops standing near me. All the guys stop what they're doing and watch as two policemen drag a young, disheveled woman by the arms. I'd seen her in the streets and at the shelters. She'd obviously been manhandled, barely able to walk, stoned, her lip bleeding.

"Naw, it ain't no good," the county jailer declares.

The boys are disappointed, so they deride her for being a piece of crap from the streets. I want to believe that the cops are real human beings behind the badges and guns, but the evidence in front of me is to the contrary. A woman officer appears and the boys straighten up. She pulls on plastic gloves and pats the woman's body and searches her pockets. She ain't playing patty-cakes either. No different from the men, she jerks the woman around like a defenseless rag doll. I imagine wrestling the cops to the ground, one by one, like the Raramuri at Semana Santa.

My arms are still locked behind my back. My arresting officer has ignored me for at least an hour. He has been chatting with two other cops who are processing their latest arrestees. Now they're mocking me, berating me for living in the streets, for not having an address to give them or a phone number or a real job. I'm tired. My bad shoulder is aching from the strain of the cuffs.

"My driver's license is valid, you have my passport, and you've seen that I have a clean record. The least you can do is take off these cuffs. I'm not a criminal." I stare into their eyes coldly and sternly. I've had enough. He promptly takes his key and unlocks the cuffs. I stretch my arms very slowly, taking every precaution to remain calm and refrain from making any movements that could be interpreted as a threat. I'm in the midst of rabid dogs, with no defense.

I explain to the magistrate what had transpired. I agree with her that to claim to know whether or not Jesus would kick the officer's ass was a little presumptive, but I emphasize that it was unnecessary for the policeman to shut down the free meal and I underline that no one was in danger, least of all the cop.

The magistrate writes me up for causing a disturbance by cursing in public. She sets my bail at $300 and informs me that a number of my friends are waiting outside and claim they have the money to bail me out. I respond that I wouldn't ask my friends to pay for something so absurd. She directs the cop to lock me up.

The jailer gruffly orders me to remove my shoestrings until it dawns on him that I'm wearing sandals. I join about twenty other men in the tank and sit on the floor. The benches are already packed.

I accept my plight with equanimity. I've been sitting on canyon rocks for four months, surrounded by snakes, scorpions, and tarantulas. The concrete floor is no big deal. I'm not sorry for what I said, nor am I upset that I'm in jail. Nothing like a night or two in jail to ground me in the good old USA. I accept my predicament as another lesson in reality, another firsthand view into the dark side of the American way of life. I'm just exactly where I need to be.

I drift away from the detention center and return to memories of Mexico and the Semana Santa celebration in Norigachi. The aroma of pine fires and incense replaces the rank odors of tight confinement; Raramuri drumbeats drown out the sleep murmurs and snores of the inmates.

Throngs of Raramuri had arrived by foot from all parts of the sierra, each group carrying flags that represented their individual communities. The women and little girls wore bright, multi-colored skirts, blouses, and head scarves, and toted baskets and clay pots, with babies tied to their backs with rebozos.

The men and boys sported huaraches, loincloths and turkey-feather headdresses, their bare torsos painted with white dots; white stripes ran across their faces, chests, arms, and legs. Their thick, callused feet looked like clubs, and their legs rippled with muscle. Black eyes stared through raccoon-like faces.

Late in the night, Susie and I had slept in the shadows of the rocks at the base of the hills—exhausted, mystified, transported. From Urique we'd traveled seven days by foot, guided by the river and the memory of a map drawn in the dirt, until we reached Norigachi high in the sierra above Batopilas. Multi-colored boulders filled the riverbed, smoothed by centuries of water flow, baked by the fiery sun, and chiseled into fantastic shapes by raging gusts of wind and sand.

Along one stretch of trail, boulders in the river dazzled white in the sun rays and soft white in the shadows of the cliffs, others mauve-colored and some black with white stripes. Set in the Urique River at the foot of sheer cliffs, the boulders are living beings. When I leaned into their silky, smooth sides hot from the sun, I could feel their sensuality and I thought the Lady of Guadalupe herself was writhing against my body. Susie knew exactly what I was saying.

By Friday morning the crowd in Norigachi had swelled to 400 or 500 people. The Raramuri women, sitting in the shade around the grounds of the Catholic iglesia, were a sea of color. The men danced, ten or twelve groups spread across the grounds, fifteen dancers or more per group. Tesguino, their cherished corn beer, waited in large ollas beside the church, ready for consumption. Later, the dancers gathered around the ollas and guzzled the beer from gourd cups.

Periodically throughout the day, a Mexican priest wearing the vestments of the Catholic Church and his Raramuri assistant with a sash strapped across his bare torso led the entire throng in processions through the Stations of the Cross. A third man accompanied them. Adorned with crepe-paper streamers and small mirrors attached to his vest, his face painted white, he danced and twirled a stick in the air like a shaman trickster, comedic relief to an otherwise somber procession.

Troupes of dancers followed the priests. Behind them, six men carried an effigy of Jesus that looked as old as if the Jesuits could have made it in the seventeenth century. Six women bore Mary. The Mother and the Son sat on crude wooden thrones. The Raramuri carted them on their shoulders with long wooden poles, while masses of women and children followed with somber reverence and dignity.

Jesus and Mary came to life among the Raramuri, awakened by the determined dancers and exuberant drummers. Susie and I followed close behind the pallbearers, our eyes filled with tears and our skin tingling with the sense of transubstantiation, the plaster effigies as palpable as the sons and daughters of the earth who supported them.

I could see their reflections in the flashing mirrors of the shaman and in his wild eyes as he danced around the thrones of Jesus and Mary. A people of uncommon strength, resolute of purpose, dancing and running and living in the wilderness of an inhospitable land. The Raramuri of the Sierra Madre are so grounded to the earth, so much a part of the earth that they appeared otherworldly.

After a loop through town, the procession ended in front of the church. Jesus and Mary were returned to the altar. The sound of drums and wooden noisemakers within the sanctuary rocked the 300-year-old church to its foundation.

Now, sitting in the floor of a jail, I reflect on the great gift that had been bestowed on Susie and me. We'd traveled for four months from the mountains of North Carolina to the Sierra Madre of northern Mexico, with adventures piled upon adventures. We'd both left Asheville with just a backpack, having no knowledge of the Raramuri or the Copper Canyon.

We'd made contact with that ancient tribe, meeting them on ground level—affording us the opportunity of observing their customs firsthand. Our friend we'd met in New Mexico had predicted that we'd travel to the times of a thousand years past. He was right. Never in all my wildest dreams had I imagined a place like the Copper Canyon.

When we had arrived in Asheville, I'd walked straight to the Badger Creek camp for the night, but I was too overawed to sleep more than a few hours. The long, dull bus rides from Mexico to Asheville had served to ground my state of wildness, but not very much. I lay under the lean-to knowing my life would never be the same, that I would never view the modern world in the same light. After having had exposure to the Raramuri culture, I'm convinced that the generic conceptions of modern and primitive have been inverted. The American way of life in its present state of wanton consumerism, which we wage wars to protect and annihilate the earth to sustain, is primitive—as in subhuman, undeveloped, savage.

For three consecutive nights, Susie and I slept beneath interstate bridges on our way to Mexico. Under the overpass at Crab Orchard, Tennessee, on a cold, rainy night, we had a ringside view of the "American Way of Life" as trucks rumbled and rumbled and rumbled across the bridge, while concrete pylons trembled on their steel girders.

The trucks, like menacing apparitions from a post-apocalyptic nightmare, were laden with consumer goods destined to be crammed into every nook and cranny of larger and larger houses, littered along the side of the road, or dumped into landfills.

How many 18-wheelers are required to supply the inordinate glut of material goods for Asheville alone?

Macabre and a thousand illusions removed from reality, this existence we call modern.

Which culture is Third World?

Which culture is primitive?

Before leaving for Mexico, I had reread *You Can't Go Home Again* by Thomas Wolfe, whose old home place sits two blocks from the jail. I thought about the fatal illusions of economic expansion based on unrestrained development. The chapters titled "Boom Town" and "The Catastrophe" are haunting accounts of the history of Asheville from 1920 to 1930. Wolfe believed that the rise and fall of Asheville's economy during that decade was a microcosm of what had transpired all across America.

By 1920, Asheville's population had grown to around 50,000; the speculators predicted it would double again by 1930, basing much of their lending and investing on those projections. Between 1920 and 1922, the number of building permits issued each year tripled, and the assessed value of city property climbed 250 percent.

But while the city fathers, the business community, and the Chamber of Commerce promised unprecedented opportunities for accumulating wealth, Wolfe saw only "a spirit of drunken waste and wild destruction [that] was everywhere apparent." With the incisive words of a prophet, he charged that the truth underneath the façade of prosperity was "greed, greed, greed—deliberate, crafty, motivated."

The chapter titled "The Catastrophe" gives a gripping account of the final disintegration, when the banks closed and the city government went bust. The economists of the day ascribed the fall to a breakdown of the capitalist system, but Wolfe proclaimed that the "ruin of Libya Hill (Asheville) was much more than the ruin of the bank and the breakdown of the economic and financial order. ... The essence of the catastrophe was the ruin of the human conscience."

Wolfe's prophecy still rings through the streets of today's Asheville, and across the entire United States of America.

I cling to the memory of the Raramuri and the simplicity of their way of life.

In the middle of the night, the jailer pushes Crazy Eddie into the bull pen. He stumbles to the bench and passes out drunk.

For years, Eddie has been a good buddy to many of the people who frequent the streets of downtown Asheville. I met him back in the days when I still had an apartment on Walnut Street. On Sunday mornings, we'd drink coffee on the bench beside the Lexington Street parking lot while he waited for the beer stores to open. Daily, he panhandles for booze. Booze makes him happy and dulls the pain in his legs. He shuffles along the streets with a cane, his legs mangled from a tour of duty in Vietnam. He's in his late fifties, yet looks like he's carrying seventy-plus years in his crinkled, pockmarked face.

One day I'd seen him sitting on a bench in front of the public library. My first impression was that he'd fallen off a motorcycle and slid about twenty feet on the pavement. His face and bald forehead were scraped raw. One of his elbows and a knee oozed blood and pus. His clothes were ripped. He wore one tennis shoe with no shoestrings, the other foot bare.

"Eddie, what the hell happened?"

"A cop pushed me." He took a swig of wine from the bottle he'd hidden in the public trash can.

"What do you mean a cop pushed you? Where?"

"We's camped under the bridge up by the Amoco, and the cops come in on us in the middle of the night. They was four of them. I was having trouble makin' it down the slide, as we call it—you know, the concrete slope. So a cop come after me, kicked my cane, and I slid all the way down to the bottom. Well, I slid and rolled. Headfirst."

I was stunned. I stared at his wounds in disbelief. I take a lot of stories I hear in the streets with a grain of salt, but Eddie ain't lying. I handed my water bottle to Delores, his friend sitting beside him, and asked her to clean the wounds as best she could. I headed towards the drugstore to buy a tube of antiseptic and some bandages. I requisitioned a friend for the money, since I didn't have any.

Later, I had visited the chief of police (he knows exactly who Crazy Eddie is) and asked him if his cop who busted the homeless camp under the bridge was okay. I told him about Eddie, and said I figured the cop was in bad shape too if he had had to protect himself against such a powerful man. The chief said his cop was fine.

Eddie struggles to a sitting position on the concrete bench in front of me. As I wait for his eyes to clear, I start laughing. "Mickey … ? Is that you?" He's struggling for comprehension, cross-eyed.

"I'm afraid so, Crazy Eddie."

"Well, I'll be goddamn."

I'm thinking about the plight of my twenty-three roommates. We're a pretty rough-looking bunch. Most appear to be drunk. Several are cut, scraped, and bruised. A couple of young guys in shorts are bemoaning every second of their party interruptus in the Buncombe County jail.

An older guy is screaming for the jailer to bring him his medication. He says, "They ain't got no right to keep my meds from me. None of us, as of yet, is convicted of nothing. None of us, as of yet, ain't stood before no judge." He slumps in his seat. "We're locked up at the word of a cop," he mumbles while sweeping his finger across the cell, wild-eyed like a prophet.

While his finger hangs in the air, a big giant of a guy farts long and loud and then shits a week's worth of cheap wine and greasy food into the toilet bowl. So far, three of my roommates have taken a shit. The shitter is in the cell, right beside us, set apart by a three-foot wall. A few guys snicker. The prophet who had been preachin' the truth about guilty until proven innocent sinks into his chair with resignation.

Bienvenidos a Asheville, Señor Mahaffey.

First, I voice my complaints about the inhuman treatment of arrestees at the Buncombe County jail directly to the police. Then, I report my experience to the county commissioners and City Council members. No one seems to care, so I write a detailed account in the *Mountain Xpress*, a popular weekly newspaper in western North Carolina.

Over the next few weeks, I ponder what measures are necessary to bring more public accountability to the powers that be. The voice of a homeless backpacker doesn't carry much sway in a tourist town where every square foot of space is an investment opportunity, with a corporate police force ready and willing to protect those investments.

On Tuesday afternoon, before City Council is called to order, the city manager approaches me and asks why I attend all these boring Council meetings when I could be at home watching a good James Bond movie. I laugh and tell him that Council meetings are much more entertaining than James Bond. (Not to mention that I don't have a home or a television; besides, what the hell is it to you? I don't say this to his face, but I think it.) He's the same guy who once warned me to tone down my rhetoric in public about city management, or "things could get brutal" for me.

It's nearing midnight by the time I reach the podium. No one else remains in chambers except the seven Council members, the city manager, clerk, attorney, and me. I know they're exhausted and not likely to pay much attention to what I have to say. However, like them, I've been in the meeting since 5 p.m.—I've paid my dues to speak for three minutes during public comment.

I report the incident that had occurred at the free meal, and describe to Council the treatment of arrestees in our community's jail. I ask them if those are calculated methods employed to sweep Asheville clean of undesirables in order to protect the city's taxpaying customer base? Council unanimously defers to the city manager.

He sits with his back to the public podium, so he has to cock his head around to glare at me. He addresses me as Mr. Mahaffey, and invites me to make an appointment to meet with him and the chief at my convenience. He reminds me that it's very late. I suggest that since the press isn't present, it's an opportune time to have a short discussion about the meanspiritedness of Clean Sweep Asheville. The city attorney shakes his head like he has no idea. The city manager is like stone. His eyes remain fixed on his legal pad. I walk away from the podium, and the mayor adjourns the meeting.

I exit Council chambers and head for Badger Creek, considering more effective ways and means to have a stronger political voice in the Asheville community.

CHAPTER NINE

Mayor From Badger Creek

Martine approaches our camp on muleback, cantering hard through the rocky creek. He jumps to the ground at a run and insists that I follow him upriver. I'm not sure why. He's on a mission, beside himself with excitement, speaking rapid-fire Spanish so I'm only able to catch a few words of his explanation.

Last New Year's Eve when I was in pueblo Munerachi, Martine appeared in town leading a massive bull by a rope. With the expertise of a master butcher and with the help of six Raramuri men, he wrestled the bull to the ground, tied his legs, slit his throat with a machete, and proceeded to cut the bull down to chunks of meat and ribs.

Later, after adding chiles, tomatoes, onions, garlic, and corn, the men dropped metal tubs brimming with stew into deep fire pits filled with rocks, covered them with sheets of tin, and cooked the hearty meal throughout the night. Early the next morning Martine honored his guest by serving me first among the throng gathered for the community feast.

So I follow him without question.

He leads his mule by a rope as we hike up the trail through a steep side canyon until we reach a flat, open area rimmed by a rock wall. Two fiddlers and three guitarists perch atop a boulder, serenading some thirty or forty Raramuri men and women gathered inside the wall, dancing and drinking. A dozen or more drums vibrate and echo through the shadowed cove. In pueblo Munerachi, throngs of Raramuri men, women and children are gathered celebrating Semana Santa, but this group is holding a private affair far removed from the other festivities.

We weave through the dancers and drummers and present ourselves to four Raramuri elders who are sitting in the shade of an arching boulder. Martine holds his cowboy hat in his hand and requests permission for his white gringo friend to be accepted within the circle, assuring them that I'm a good guy and that I had stayed up all night with the Raramuri last New Year's Eve. He's very polite and respectful with his request to the old men. Same as me, he's a chabochi to the Raramuri, an outsider.

The elders never flinch, maintaining the same pose they'd had before we abruptly appeared in their presence. They offer no sign that they even see the two of us standing in front of them, the same as the woman at the top of the mountain when Susie and I were lost in the snowstorm. Undeterred, Martine patiently awaits their verdict.

"Cinco." Finally one of the men holds up five fingers, but that's all he says. Five.

Martine grabs my arm and pulls me towards a large clay olla at the edge of the field. He dips a gourd cup into the pot and motions for me to drink. I take tentative sips from the potent brew. I'd tasted tesguino at the first Semana Santa ceremony I attended in Norigachi, but this isn't corn beer. This is raw agave, moonshine tequila. Martine reprimands me for my timidity, instructing me to drain the whole cup.

He dips the gourd again and holds the brimming cup to my mouth. I drain it to a chorus of "Eso! Eso!" from a handful of curious observers, and then I down another and another until I've finished five full cups.

"Cinco, gringo. Bien hecho!" Martine beams with satisfaction, his mission accomplished. I'd fulfilled the requirements of their initiation, and now I'm welcomed into the inner circle.

With tequila burning my gullet like liquid fire, seeping into my belly and all the way to my feet, three drummers surround me, banging their drums, laughing. "Baile, gringo!"

I dance and dance, fully absorbed in the presence of the moment with my new companions and their secluded hideaway deep in the wild canyon. The drummers never leave my side. If I attempt to rest, they taunt me and increase the tempo of their drumbeats. My whole body pulsates with the vibrations of the quivering deerskins, the noise ringing in my ears.

Finally, late in the night, totally exhausted, my legs like rubber, I manage to slip away unnoticed and stumble along the pitch-black trail until I reach our camp by the river. My friends are snuggled close to a bed of dying embers, sound asleep. Sporadic drumbeats reverberate across the river while dancers, in silhouette at the edge of the bluff, pitch birdcalls through the gorge.

The strident drone of croaking bullfrogs rises from the muck of the riverbank, millions of frogs filling the narrow canyon with love songs, their passion resounding up and down the rivers of the entire Sierra Madre range. I'm mesmerized by the hypnotic cadence, an almost eerie sound like the earth is projecting her soul from the antediluvian age.

A band of Raramuri on the other side of the river toss more logs to the fire, causing sparks to dance into the air over the bluff. Then a second group further upriver and a third group on the hill behind our camp follow suit, until the whole ravine is filled with firelight.

The group across the river suddenly projects a startling burst of drumbeats, and the other two groups follow in succession as more sparks shoot into the air, as if the pulse of the deerskins is stoking the flames to greater heights. They pound their drums with a manic fury, and then the drums of the first group cease and the other two follow in turn until the sound of the river and the frogs prevail.

Chills shiver through my body and my eyes fill with tears, so awesome is the natural music. Before my adrenalin has subsided, all three groups resume, banging their drums in unison until the resurgent sounds roll like waves through the canyon.

Water rushing over river rock, three bands of drums, croaking frogs, and crackling fires in harmonic convergence, creating the distinct rhythms of a symphony orchestra. I hear the individual chords of violins, tympani, trombones, trumpets, clarinets, oboes, and viola.

Have the Raramuri learned how to harmonize their drums with the natural resonance of the elements and create songs that seem to flow from the beginning of creation?

Or am I hallucinating from the tequila and the trance dance with the Raramuri?

So captivated by the mystifying sounds, I hadn't even noticed my travel companions sitting up in their sleeping bags, eyes wide with wonder, witnessing the same phenomena as me.

But how could I pull it off, I ask myself?

Just walk out the door, I answer, just as I'd done in so many other situations since I'd first heard David shout those priceless words at Vincent's Ear.

I don't hesitate. I dress, pack my gear and walk into downtown. According to the clock at Five Points Restaurant, it's 3:30 a.m. I stash my backpack behind a hedgerow and pick up litter along the curbs and clean up around the public trash cans while I mull over my new political aspirations. The current mayor of Asheville is a Jewish woman from the North. Not a small thing in a Southern, mountain town of 70,000 people, where many are still struggling to adjust to equal rights for non-Aryans and women.

Would the citizens of Asheville elect a mayor who's considered a homeless man, without a real job or means of transportation? Without a telephone or the internet? I'm sure I don't have a chance in hell of winning, yet there are significant members of our community whose voices need to be heard in order to keep our community balanced, so that the vitality of Asheville is not snuffed out by hyperaggressive development.

Earlier, I had arisen from my sleeping bag like I'd been jolted by an electric shock. I thought I had heard a distinct voice coming from the forest. I had no idea of the time or where I was camped. No cacti-studded mountains rising from the Urique River, no mesquite trees buzzing with bees, nor the sweet aroma of orange blossoms. No drums, singing frogs, or bonfires—only the gurgling brook at Badger Creek and a cluster of white pines in Asheville, North Carolina.

I took a deep breath, slowly coming to consciousness, remembering that I'd left the canyons five days ago. I stoked the fire and set a pot of water to boil, trying to recall the source of the voice that had awakened me so abruptly. Now I remember: "Run for mayor of Asheville." Those are the words I heard as clear as the popping fire, strong words that rattled me from a deep, deep sleep. Was I dreaming, or did I hear a voice from the dark forest? Regardless, the idea is etched in my mind and I can't dismiss it.

For several years I've been as involved as any private citizen in our city's governmental affairs, but I've never considered running for political office—swore I never would. As absurd as the notion appears on the surface, I can't ignore my most intimate instincts. I've learned countless times that if I listen to my inner urgings without question, I will be led in a good and necessary way.

Okay, I'll run for the office of the mayor of Asheville, speaking the words aloud to hear their sounds and to better grasp exactly what I'm contemplating. I will organize a creative, grassroots campaign that will bring honor to community politics and stay true to the good spirit so manifest in Asheville. Memories of the Raramuri and my observations of their commitment to their own community will inform my decisions. Images of their powerful canyons will inspire my steps. Living with very few material possessions, the Raramuri manifest strength of character and a sweetness of disposition seldom witnessed in the industrialized world. In that spirit, we will campaign like we're going to City Hall.

At dawn, a lieutenant with the Asheville Police Department rolls beside me in his unmarked patrol car and wishes me a good morning. He asks where I've been, claims he'd been keeping an eye out for me for several days. At first I'm not sure what he means. Some of our confrontations in the streets have been less than friendly, but of all things, he invites me to the annual police banquet at the Civic Center to receive a community-service award.

He claims he'd submitted my nomination to the chief of police and that the chief had agreed. I'm flabbergasted. Why would the police reward their most vocal critic? Regardless of their intent, I don't hesitate. I promise to be at the banquet, honored that they would even consider me for the award.

I answer a few of his questions about my last excursion to Mexico, and then I lean against the door of his car and reveal my political plans. He guffaws with laughter and says he'll look forward to the show. The campaign for mayor of Asheville has officially commenced.

At eight o'clock I wait for Beth Trigg in front of her workplace. If I'm to build a credible campaign with a voice that will rise above the slander, mockery and indifference a man who lives out of a backpack is sure to draw, I will need someone of Beth's caliber and reputation to manage our efforts. We will need to organize a group of workers who are sensitive to all the parts of the body of our community, especially those who have been most neglected: the poor, women, people of color, the elderly, and the mentally ill. Each individual part of the body is ineffective on its own, but in accord with all the other parts, the whole is balanced and fluid.

I've been aware for several years of Beth's involvement in other grassroots efforts as an activist and a writer. She has a brilliant mind, a true voice for the voiceless, and boundless energy. Also, since I'm not connected to the grid in any form, I'll need someone adept at communications.

After explaining to her that our campaign must be a purely grassroots effort and that no one will be paid for their work, Beth volunteers without a moment's hesitation. When Allie Morris comes on board, the synergy of our campaign rises. She's only nineteen, but exudes a creative energy seldom seen in persons much older. Around town she wears a T-shirt that reads "Mahaffey for Mayor" on the front, and "I'm serious!" on the backside.

I'm sitting under the gazebo at Pritchard Park considering essential themes for the campaign. Lying on the bench beside me are my copies of a biography of Che Guevarra and a collection of essays by Vaclav Havel. Last night at Badger Creek I read by candlelight until late in the evening, contemplating the nature of revolution and the courage of revolutionaries who effect dramatic change against seemingly insurmountable odds. I scrutinize the differences between Che's armed revolt in Cuba and Havel's Velvet Revolution in Czechoslovakia, both exemplary studies in courage and determination.

Once, I stood in Wencelaus Square in Old Town Prague and tried to imagine the events of the Velvet Revolution in 1989, when the Czech dissidents toppled the Communist regime without returning violence for violence. They jangled 300,000 key chains simultaneously, and the walls of domination crumbled to the ground. Vaclav Havel, who for decades had been one of the primary activists of the underground opposition movement, had inspired thousands—if not millions—of outsiders with his declaration that: "Communism was not defeated by military force, but by life, by the human spirit, by conscience, by the resistance of Being and man to manipulation."

When the Czech dissidents first tasted freedom after decades of isolation behind the Iron Curtain, they looked towards the West for inspiration and guidance, only to discover that the Western culture as a whole had become as demoralized by the dictatorship of gross consumerism and mindless living as they had been under Communist rule. Havel tagged the paradox as "the new totalitarianism of consumption, commerce, and money."

I have been a student of the Velvet Revolution for many years and have been greatly inspired by the intense commitment of a handful of dissidents—mainly artists, actors, intellectuals, musicians, students, and common workers—who kept the dreams of freedom alive in the Prague underground. Many of them were jailed numerous times, ostracized, and forced underground.

Despite the severity of their oppression, the revolutionaries decided, as articulated by Havel, to "Resist by speaking the truth simply because it was the right thing to do, without speculating whether it would lead somewhere tomorrow, or the day after, or ever. ... At the very least it meant that someone was not supporting the government of lies."

Those words have informed all my political activism in Asheville. When speaking for the poor, the authorities seldom listen. In a culture built on consumerism, protests against air pollution fall on deaf ears. To call for budget restraint in a boom-time economy is often discounted, if not outright reviled. Yet the realities of the destructive nature of the American way of life must be specifically named and alternative measures offered.

There's very little I can do personally to resist the domination of the powerful over the powerless in the world at large. Only in my own neighborhood and community can I hope to make a difference. It's easy to hurl invectives from afar, not so easy to confront the realities in our own backyard. Besides, Asheville is a microcosm of the greater state and nation. The corporate dynamics of city government at root level are the same as in Washington. I understand the abuses of corporate military power by observing local, corporate police. I comprehend the plight of the downtrodden worldwide from what I witness in the streets of my hometown.

I spend the day picking up litter and handing out voter-registration forms to the homeless and the young people eighteen or older who hang out downtown. I meet two homeless veterans of the Vietnam War who had never registered to vote and probably never would've registered, except that they view me as one of their own. They'd heard stories of how I had spoken on their behalf at City Council on many occasions, and they'd read some of my commentaries in the newspapers. I may have to remind them several times, even take them to the polling booths; nonetheless, I'm sure they will vote Mahaffey for mayor.

Mike only needed to register in our county. A lifetime voter, he willingly completed the necessary paperwork. He has recovered some since I saw him sitting under a bridge at daybreak. He was so inebriated then I couldn't have imagined he'd still be on his feet this afternoon. The endurance of the drinkers is phenomenal. Drunk early in the morning and drunker in the middle of the day. In the evening they're still standing, panhandling for spare change, staggering to the convenience store for another bottle. For weeks at a stretch.

Last week I saw him stumble into Malaprop's when the place was packed with patrons. His clothes were ragged nasty. When he bumped into a newspaper rack and nearly fell to the floor, I rushed to assist him, knowing that if I didn't take action the police would.

As I grasped his arm, I realized his clothes were smeared with fresh feces. I led him outside the bookstore, barely able to stifle my gag reflexes, and offered him a clean pair of sweatpants and a T-shirt I had in my pack. He was ornery as hell, grumbling every step of the way, but I finally managed to coax him into the bathroom at the public library.

When he returned, he handed me his shit-smeared clothes in a plastic bag and headed up the stairs. Like an afterthought, he remembered I had been waiting for him and mumbled, "I'll see ya later. I need a drink."

He left, and I went looking for the same.

I don't have any luck with Sammy. He's trashed. I need to catch him early in the morning before he commences his manic frenzy to acquire crack cocaine. Yesterday I saw him sitting on a bench, fried on crack, his feet bloodied from racing through the streets in ill-fitting shoes, begging for more money. In the mornings he recognizes me as his friend; in the afternoon he has no idea who I am. My friends and I dressed his wounds and pleaded with him to come to our camp to heal. He refused. As soon as we left, he limped up the sidewalk begging for more change.

I can't write off these guys as mere statistics culled from the police blotter, or pieces of litter to be swept out of sight. Nor can I dismiss them as collateral damage in the embattled trenches of capitalism. Granted, serving those in the clutches of mental, physical, and emotional desperation is no easy task. All who have grappled with alcoholism and drug addiction know that the worst times are marked by belligerence, intimidation, rudeness, and outright danger. Yet other times, these same people display a profound sweetness and purity of soul, enriching the community with stories and wisdom that both confound and delight.

And they deserve to vote—as much so as the businessman who hides his addictions behind closed doors.

In an interview for my candidate profile, the reporter with the daily newspaper asks what I do for a living and I promptly respond that I'm a professional litter-picker-upper. She convinces me to phrase my work as a community-service volunteer so that I might be taken more seriously. I understand, and I do want to be taken seriously, I tell her, but my self-appointed role as litter man is a job I'm very proud of.

At street level, I'm able to observe firsthand the realities of life downtown. When I first learned about Clean Sweep Asheville, the city's plan to remove the homeless and idle from the downtown shopping areas, I began to report my observations through City Council and commentaries in the local papers. Soon I became a regular at Council, and now I've attended countless meetings concerning the city budget, air pollution, personnel, mass transit, police, garbage, and water. As a result, I've gained a self-conferred degree in civic affairs.

I return to my camp at Badger Creek anticipating a night of solitude in the woods to rest and gather my thoughts for the upcoming candidates forums. I scurry into the bushes around the camp, making sure I'm not detected. I can see the headlines now: Mayoral Candidate Charged With Trespassing. It's always necessary that I stay inconspicuous, but the stakes are even higher now. As soon as I reach the lean-to, I realize something is wrong. Nothing is where I left it. I raise the flap on the lean-to. All of my gear is gone! My backpack, sleeping bag, tarp, poncho, cooking pots, cup, spoon, extra clothes. Everything. All my possessions have disappeared.

For the next several days I'm at a complete loss. Granted, my possessions are meager; still, they are the makings of my home and I don't have the money to replace them. I sleep on the couch at Beth Trigg's house and have a difficult time staying focused on the campaign. In all the years I've been living outside, no one has ever stolen my gear. I attempt to shrug it off, but I retain a deep sense of loss and disorientation.

Several days later, while on my way to check on my camp, I happen to notice through the bushes by the creek what appears to be a blue tarp a little distance from my place. I'd never seen anyone camping in the area, and I know where most of the camps in town are located.

I swerve from the sidewalk and peer into the undergrowth. Trails of smoke waft from the dying embers of a campfire. I listen for signs of life but don't see or hear anyone, so I ease closer for a better view.

There's no doubt the water pot sitting on a rock by the fire pit is mine. I bought it in Mexico. Then I spot a young guy lying atop a sleeping bag under the tarp. I crawl through a gap in the brush and he jumps to attention, startled. I hold my hands in the air to demonstrate that I'm not a threat. I introduce myself, and explain that I live down the creek and happened see the tarp as I was passing by. As I sit by the fire pit talking to the kid, I recognize the sleeping bag as mine, and then my backpack and all the rest of my missing gear.

We enjoy a friendly chat about living outdoors and how difficult it's been as of late with the cops cracking down so hard on the homeless. I suggest that he had better camouflage his camp because if I can see his tarp, so can the police. He claims he's just turned eighteen and that he's been homeless for two years because neither of his divorced parents wanted him to live with them. His story is pathetic, like so many others I hear almost every day, yet he's a very endearing kid so my anger subsides.

After a pause in our conversation, I reveal that most of the gear I see in his campground is mine.

He stutters a quick response about how he'd found my camp and thought it was abandoned and that the former camper had left the gear. Tears well in his eyes, and I notice his hands are shaking. I allay his fears of a reprisal and make a deal to let him keep everything except for the backpack and the sleeping bag. And the water pot from Mexico. He has other blankets for the time being and sufficient time to find another sleeping bag before cold weather sets in.

I leave Jesse's camp with my most essential gear, a new friend, and his signature on a voter-registration form.

On the day of the first candidates' forum in West Asheville, it dawns on me that I haven't even thought about a campaign wardrobe. All I have are the shorts I'm wearing and two T-shirts—the only clothes that survived two months in the canyons. I don't even have one pair of socks. I practice good hygiene, but still . . . .

At Malaprop's, I meet my friend Peruvio and explain my dilemma. He rushes to his apartment nearby and returns with a beautiful navy-blue shirt that fits me perfectly. I take a city bus to the Goodwill store and buy a pair of pants for four dollars, and then take the next bus to the forum. In the bus I notice that the pants I'd bought are women's pants! Right before the speeches begin, I whisper to Beth and the other supporters that I'm wearing girl pants. They're impressed.

Four current Council members are on the mayoral ticket. They have trouble with the two- to three-minute time allotments to elaborate their platforms. In Council meetings they are allowed to speak without time constraints. I'd been trained at Council meetings by the three-minute limit imposed on citizens who speak during the public-comment period. I know exactly when the red light on the podium will flash. I'd learned to say a whole lot in a very short amount of time, and the same for several candidates for a seat on City Council. Our comments on current issues are right on target.

The following morning on a local conservative radio show, a group of political observers said my presentation was impressive; however, they did suggest I consider a different wardrobe.

On September 11, all campaigning comes to an abrupt halt. Our city mourns with the nation and the world after the terrorist attacks. The next day, a friend and I begin a two-day prayer walk from downtown Asheville to the western edge of Madison County, about forty miles away. Over the past few years I've taken many walking journeys to center myself and gain renewed inspiration for continuing my commitment to service. We only carry a blanket and a tarp, but the weight of the terror and ominous foreboding of more death to come make it the most burdensome walk I'd ever made.

The crisp beauty of the early fall day wants to inspire us, but in reality the first breath of fall seems a contradiction to the reality of our world tragedy. After reaching Madison County, we sit beside the fire for two more days, strengthening our resolve to face the work that awaits us in the days to come.

When we return to town, it's clear that the time of mourning and reflection has come to an end. Now sabers are rattling in the land of the free and the home of the brave, razor-honed to execute the Lord's vengeance.

While we're walking door-to-door canvassing for votes, we hear the news that the United States has invaded Afghanistan and is obliterating every living thing for hundreds of miles. Code name: Operation Infinite Justice.

On the day of the elections, we carry voters to the polls in the back of Beth Trigg's pickup. Jesse and two men in their late fifties who live in the streets cast their votes for the first time in their lives. The two older guys had never even registered before. They claim we're the only people who'd ever stood up for them, and for them alone all the work and challenges of the campaign have been worth the effort. When they exit the polling booth, they're so proud they're about to burst their shirt buttons. Jesse swaggers out of the precinct and gives me a high five.

We await the results from the Board of Elections with a host of friends and supporters at Beanstreets Coffeehouse. I've never been a part of a more diverse amassing of people: young and old, rich and penniless, men, women and children, black and white, Democrat and Republican. When the finals are announced, many of our supporters are deeply disappointed. At first we hear we'd garnered a little over 800 votes. We gather in a circle inside the café, and one by one they express their feelings about the campaign and vow to continue working to see that our platform is represented in the coming years. By the time we're finished, we receive word that in the final tally we had earned the confidence of 1,000 voters.

Exactly 1,000.

I couldn't have been more thrilled or more proud of our efforts. With a true grassroots effort, little money, no TV or radio exposure, a candidate who lives out of a backpack, and a group of very talented campaigners, we'd won nearly a tenth of the total votes, far beyond our critics' estimations. Our efforts won't even earn a footnote in Asheville's history, but we'd spoken for the voiceless of our community, and 1,000 voices had been heard.

As soon as the new mayor is inaugurated, I break camp and head for Canyon Urique.

CHAPTER TEN

Holy Devils On A Mission

I halfheartedly resist the young Raramuri man's offer of tesguino; still he refuses to take no for an answer. I take a good swig from the jug and then a second at his insistence, but no more for now, I plead. I can barely swallow the heady brew so early in the morning. His name is Alvaro. He laughs at every word I speak, pulls his buddies closer so they can laugh at the big gringo's broken Spanish. He's zooming like the party started days ago, like he's so stoked for the Semana Santa dance he can hardly contain the energy in his slight frame of a body.

"Vamos a pintar arête. Vas a pintar usted?" He whispers in my ear like he's telling a secret, and with great flourishes traces marks and circles on my chest and arms. Before I can question him further about the day's events he sprints around the church twirling his matraca, a small wooden noisemaker that makes a clicking sound when spun. He's quick as lightning.

I understand that the diablos are going to get painted soon, but is he inviting me to paint? I'm not sure. I know the tradition of the Raramuri is to cover their bodies with paint for the Easter dance, as I'd witnessed in Norigachi and Munerachi, so I assume that's what he's saying.

Breathless, Alvaro returns to my side, raises my arm in the air, and yells like if he does, I'll understand: "Si, tu vas a pintar."

I'm going to help paint the others—or get painted? I understand his Spanish words but I still don't understand his intent. Surely the proud Raramuri would never invite an outsider to participate in the dance, especially a gringo, not at Semana Santa. I only count three men among the group milling around behind the church who appear to be non-Raramuri. The Raramuri refer to outsiders as chabochis, literally "whiskered ones." And I have a beard!

"Vamos!"

About thirty men, a few women, and three children hurriedly leave pueblo Guadalupe Coronado and race up the hill overlooking the town. Alvaro clutches my arm and pulls me along with them.

"Vamonos, gringo. Es tiempo pintar!" The time to get painted has arrived. I hustle after them, having no idea where we're headed or what will happen when we arrive; however, I'm on the trail hanging close to Alvaro, so exhilarated by the totally unexpected invitation my feet hardly touch the ground.

"El sol es muy fuerte. Descansamos," states the young man at the front of our troupe.

We've kept a swift pace across the mountain ledges on a trail high above the Urique River. My legs are strong from six weeks of hiking in the canyons, but I'm content to rest and calm my adrenalin. We sit quietly beside a cluster of boulders, shaded from the blistering sun. Some of the men stare at me and smile warmly, their rich brown skin glowing in the subdued light.

"Vas pintar, gringo?" The teenaged boy asks expectantly.

"Espero que si." I tentatively respond that I hope so, but I don't know for sure. How can I tell him that to do so would surpass my wildest dreams?

The young guy sitting beside him flashes a smile, "Raramuri, Mexicanos y un gringo. Todos juntos."

"Si, que muy bueno, amigo!" I'm bowled over by the gleam in his eyes and the childlike simplicity of his acknowledgment that three separate races of people are participating together, and I'm proud as a peacock to be counted among them.

Three ancient Raramuri women sit on a rock wall beside the adobe house where the painting ceremony is to take place. They're so tiny I think a puff of wind could blow them over the edge of the rocky cliffs. I can't imagine how old they are or what stories the deep wrinkles in their faces could tell. They hold their scarves over their mouths to conceal their giggles, like little girls, seemingly as excited for this year's Semana Santa as the many, many others they've attended in their long lives.

But there's no hint of a breeze on the cliffs. The noontime sun is blazing hot as hell into the Urique canyon, and the few scraggly trees provide little shade.

I stand alone at the edge of the group, uncertain of what to do next. The other men spread around the grounds in pairs, remove their shirts, dip their hands into buckets of black paint, and begin smearing the goo over their shoulders and legs. A roly-poly Raramuri man totes a large corn sack from group to group collecting each man's clothes, recording the names and the items in a notebook, and promising to care for them until the end of the ceremony.

Alvaro pulls me towards an elder who holds a carved stick in his hand like a wand. The elder, with a deeply wrinkled face and a quiet and subdued demeanor, asks if I would like to serve as a diablo.

"Si, senor, con permiso." I enthusiastically nod my head.

He taps my shoulders and the top of my head with the wand, lifts it in the air towards each of the cardinal directions, and offers the stick to me. As instructed, I point the wand to the four directions exactly as he had done and then genuflect. That's it. I'm officially ordained in the Raramuri tradition and granted permission to dance as a diablo. I remove my shirt and cap and place them in the sack with the caretaker. I borrow a knife and cut the legs from my jeans.

I'd been to Holy Week with the Raramuri on three previous journeys in other parts of the canyons, but only as an observer. I'd never imagined an invitation to join in the dance. Can I possibly keep pace with world-class athletes like the Raramuri, who are world-renowned for their almost superhuman endurance?

I overheard one man say that the Semana Santa dance is as physically challenging as the fifty-mile marathon held each year in Urique. I ran track and cross-country in high school and college and continued running long distances for years. I've walked thousands of miles on the trails of my Appalachian homeland and have years' worth of canyon walking in my legs, yet I know the marathon dance will be the challenge of a lifetime.

Butterflies churn in my stomach, eliciting a memory from high school when I was waiting for the baton to run my leg of the mile relay at the state championships in Raleigh, the last event of the meet. Our team's victory depended on my performance. Our team carried away the championship trophy. Hopefully I can last the course with the elite athletes from Canyon Urique.

Alvaro, still laughing hysterically, escorts me to the front of a small adobe hut where a very old Raramuri man stands beside four ollas filled to the brim with tesguino. He dips the gourd cup into the clay pot and motions for me to drink. I hold the cup above my head and again acknowledge the four directions. I take a few sips and hand the cup to the elder. He vigorously shakes his head and orders me to drink it all. In my excitement I had forgotten my lesson from Munerachi when I drank the agave moonshine.

I drain the beer, wipe the residue from my beard, and grunt with satisfaction as I'd seen the others do. Delighted, they motion for others to come and watch the giant gringo drink their cherished brew. The corn mash courses through my body like fire.

"Puro tesguino, puro maize!"

"Que rico!" I exclaim.

"Eso! Eso!" They rejoin.

They had planted the corn on the sides of the cliffs in rocky fields nearly vertical to the canyon floor during the month of June when the temperatures reach 120 degrees. They'd shucked the ears, shelled the corn with their hands, and ground the kernels for three days in stone metates. The men had gathered huge piles of firewood and stirred the brew over blazing fires day and night for a week. For the Raramuri of the Sierra Madre, tesguino represents the continuation of civilization and is the fruit of arduous labor.

With black paint made from ground charcoal, and white from chalk rock, our troupe transforms into diablos. A man of my age, with black hair streaked silver and tied with a red scarf, works black paste into my cheeks and forehead, even my eyelids and ear lobes. He vigorously massages it into my beard, chest hair, and armpits. With a sculptor's intent he prepares my upper torso with a thick, charcoal base that grips to my body like a second skin.

"Todo cuerpo," the young boy explains to the novice. A white giant and a tiny wisp of a boy, maybe eleven years old, brown-skinned, eyes sparkling with wonder. Every inch of my body must be covered, he insists. As soon as the black paint dries, he traces circles of white like racoon tails on my arms and legs, and stripes like streaks of lightning on my chest. The older man stripes my baldpate, back, and chest, and draws white circles around my nipples, belly button, and eyes.

My painters step back to admire their work. They give me their sign of approval, smiling from ear to ear, obviously proud of their gringo work of art. I survey the grounds, admiring the unique styles of the other diablos, and am impressed by their diligence and care to design their dramatic costumes with earth paint and fingers. No more brown skin or white. Our identities are hidden behind the imposing masks of the diablo.

"Baile, gringo diablo. Baile!" After another round of beer, my painters direct me towards the circle of dancers.

I watch their thick, callused feet as we snake in tight figure eights, close together, nearly touching. The high-pitched tenor of the deerskin drums and the steps of our feet are synchronized with the rhythm of our heartbeats. We step and shuffle to the simple riffs of two guitars and two violins, while sun fire blazes earth paint into our skin. A cloud of dust hovers around our feet, and our yelps reverberate through the canyon walls.

The liquid corn fires my legs to dance like I'd danced with the Raramuri all my life. Drums pounding, matracas clicking like grasshoppers, whistles blowing, and reed flutes whistling. A young Raramuri hands me a wooden carved gun painted blue with streaks of white, and I tap the stock on the hard ground, mimicking the other dancers. A nail holds five small pieces of round metal in the tip of the gun, creating the sound of a den of rattlesnakes as we dance and shake in cadence with the simple chords of the guitar and fiddle.

The energy of the dancers continues to rise as the appointed hour approaches. Alvaro is racing through the throng of diablos, twirling his matraca and whooping with reckless abandon. He whoops patting his hand to his lips, followed by a derisive-sounding ha ha ha. The others follow suit.

I imitate my companeros, but neglect to pat my hand to my mouth. Alvaro rushes to correct me, taking my hand and forcing me to thump my lips. It quickly becomes apparent that every small detail of their traditions must be followed precisely.

"Con mano, gringo! Con mano!" Several other diablos look on as I whoop properly.

Suddenly, three men appear carrying the six-foot straw effigy of Judas Iscariot and lean it against the side of the house. In

Guadalupe they had referred to him as Judas, but now I hear them calling him Papa. He's dressed in Western clothes like a gringo farmer, with a pack of cigarettes in one hand, a beer can in the other. A ten-inch, hand-carved wooden phallus is attached to his waist. In Raramuri mythology Papa is the agent of misfortune, yet is God's elder brother to whom it's necessary to concede homage.

However the diablos shout in derision, slapping Judas's phallus and making jokes.

"Papa, muy grande. Muy duro!" Alvaro yells. Roars of laughter erupt from the crowd.

"Papa, muy rico, la gente muy pobre!" An older, very somber Raramuri shouts with a trailing ha ha ha tinged with mockery. Papa is very rich, the people are very poor, he cries.

"Presidente George Bush, malo cabron! Whoop, whoop, whoop ... ha ha ha!" As I shout I wonder if they even know who George Bush is.

As if prompted by a stage manager hidden behind the curtains, a man and a woman enter the yard with a piece of cardboard. With a long hunting knife, they carve a round hat and fit it with a brim. The woman kneels to the ground, dips her finger in the black paint, and scrawls GW Bush on the face of the hat. With hat in hand, she moves towards the effigy with the air of one who's performing a sacred duty and places the cardboard hat on the head of Judas Iscariot, leaving me with the sense that they had included the hat in the script from the beginning.

I can't believe what I'm witnessing. For one, I said George, not GW. They know exactly who he is and know to place the hat on Judas Iscariot, the commonly accepted Christian icon of the betrayal of all that is good and noble. We'll carry Judas on our shoulders and he will dance with the diablos, race with us through the Stations of the Cross, and be mocked and ridiculed throughout the night. I'd been questioned numerous times about the war in Afghanistan and Iraq, and was yet to meet a single soul in favor of the American invasion.

Following the advise of my companeros, I seek shade to rest while the others put the finishing touches on their masks. For a moment I have time to reflect on what I've committed to do. Just a few hours ago at the break of dawn, I'd climbed the bluff from my camp by the river to prepare myself for the day's events, not in the least expecting to be invited to paint with Raramuri diablos.

The paint grips my skin and body hair, yet I still find it hard to believe that I've been allowed into the inner circle. I remember Semana Santa in Munerachi when the frogs, the river, and a band of drums made harmony like a symphony orchestra, and how I so wanted to be accepted in the Raramuri community.

And the first time in Norigachi with Susie, when we arrived after four months of exploring the Copper Canyon with over 600 miles of walking under our belt. With tears of gratitude for having been allowed to witness the grandeur of such an unexpected event, I knew in my heart that the Raramuri would be a major part of the rest of my life.

At dawn this morning when I arrived in town, I sat on the rock wall beside the church, ready before all others for the beginning of the ceremony. As the sun peeked over the cliffs an elder entered the courtyard, unlocked the doors of the church, genuflected, and entered the sanctuary.

Two young girls wearing bright Raramuri colors and huaraches with new leather laces crisscrossed on their calves swept the steps to the church with straw brooms, their glowing faces framed by red and yellow scarves. Their twinkling eyes belied their excitement that the big day had finally arrived.

A group of men constructed pine-bough arches to form three Stations of the Cross, signifying the path of the suffering Jesus. One is placed near the church and one at each end of town. Two men climbed a rickety wooden ladder to the roof of the church and adorned the steeple with bouquets of flowers. Raramuri women in flamboyant skirts, blouses, and head scarves spread across the grounds, sweeping the dirt clean of rocks and sticks. A cluster of men struggled down the trail from the mountains, toting ollas filled with tesguino.

The Jesuit church was constructed in the late seventeenth century, when the missionaries came into the canyons to proselytize the Raramuri of the Urique canyon. Wildly ambitious priests scaled the treacherous cliffs into a harsh and mysterious land filled with a strange tribe of primitives dwelling in caves and crude huts. I couldn't disagree more with the doctrine of the Jesuits, yet I'm intrigued to imagine their reactions to the ways of the Raramuri: love of tesguino, worship of Father Sun and Mother Moon, endurance for long-distance running, enthusiasm for wrestling and kick ball, belief that after death one becomes a star in the heavens.

School buildings, a basketball court, a small community building, an infirmary, a store, and six houses comprise the flat area around the church, soon to be filled with hundreds of Mexicans, a handful of tourists, and throngs of Raramuri—many of whom are descending the cliffs in the early hours. About a dozen houses dot the hills around the pueblo, but most of the Raramuri live further upriver and in the mountains surrounding Guadalupe. For some families, the walk to town is a three- to four-hour journey.

This morning I imagined the pueblo filled with colorful Raramuri and other Mexicans from Urique, Mescalera, Naranjo, Cuauhetemoc, and Chihuahua, come to see the great battle between good and evil, see the diablos wrestle with the soldiers as Mary and Jesus are shrouded in smoke of incense. And those who know the Raramuri will recognize the symbols of Father Sun and Mother Moon, the brother of God bearing a wooden phallus, and offerings of corn beer to all of creation.

The diablos are like a herd of wild stallions champing at the bit to dash into town. The four musicians lead the way up the trail followed by a diablo carrying Papa Judas on his shoulders. We dance across the ridges, black and white paint glistening on the muscles of our legs and thighs. After three hours of painting and dancing, the diablos are stoked for the main event. So we begin the hour-long dance procession through the inner canyon seething with heat.

Our jefe, leader of the diablo dancers, is wearing blue jeans and a light-blue shirt and carries a long, wooden staff. His face is painted like a raccoon.

Three shoot ahead of the pack. "Todos juntos!" The jefe shouts with authority. Stay together! The three wayward ones slink back to the procession and we shuffle closer to the musicians, dancing in tandem.

We rest in the shade to escape the potency of the sun. They say rest, but the musicians continue playing and we continue dancing in front of them. Alvaro cautions me to pace myself, "La noche is muy largo." It's going to be a long night, and the sun is very strong. I don't heed his words. My legs are spry to the dance. The honor of being counted among the Raramuri diablos stokes the fires within me. Fierce heat, potent maize, primitive music, frenzied dancing, and thirty-two companeros aflame with energy.

Our jefe gives the signal. Over thirty black-and-white diablos charge into the throng of bystanders with drums, matracas, whistles, reed flutes, four musicians, and Judas Iscariot with a GW Bush hat. Four or five hundred people crowd the path through the pueblo, cameras flashing. We pound our wooden guns on the concrete basketball court in unison, the rumbling like rolling thunder. Little kids clutch their mothers' skirts. We yelp and whoop like madmen when the long procession of reverent believers passes by us, bearing the effigies of Mary and Jesus.

I'm nearly a foot taller than the other diablos, so I'm not difficult to spot in the crowd. One of my friends from Urique nearly faints when he recognizes me. He literally rubs his eyes like he's seeing a ghost, while his mother covers her face and peeks through her fingers. I think she's in shock from the unimaginable idea of her gringo friend painted like a diablo. I dance towards the opposite end of town in a state of pure hilarity. Alvaro and I look at each other and cannot contain our laughter.

As we approach the first Station of the Cross, the diablos sprint in two lines down the sides of the grounds—about a thirty-yard stretch—and race through the pine-bough arches. We regroup and dance through town for two more loops, each time running at full speed as we near the arches. As we pass the door of the church a group of diablos creeps up the steps, pointing their wooden guns at the women who guard the door. The Raramuri women shoo them away with stern demeanors, shouting, "No entre! No entre!"

The jefe halts our procession in front of a small adobe hut with a roof made of palm fronds. The musicians sit on a log bench and continue playing. The jefe drags a clay olla filled with tesguino from the shed and commences to serve the diablos, beginning with the musicians. My throat is parched from the dust and the potent sun, but the corn beer revives my energy. Without a rest we dance in front of the shed, drinking more tesguino until we're called upon to make another loop through town.

When the sun drops behind the mountains, a wave of cool air sweeps through the pueblo, inspiring us to dance and run with even more gusto.

It's almost dark before I pay attention to the other procession. A young Raramuri man with straight black hair tied with a yellow headband, wearing a red flannel shirt rolled to his elbows, blue jeans, and huaraches, carries the cross at the front of the procession. The cross is made from a roughhewn log that must be eighteen feet long and very heavy. The man shows little strain in his face; however he is very focused on his task, leaning on his heels for balance, the muscles in his forearms rippling.

Four Raramuri women carry the throne of Mary on wooden poles and two men carry Jesus. The Mother and the Son are adorned with crowns and robes. A group of women, young and old, walk close to the thrones, chanting prayers and waving incense. The intoxicating scent of achiote drifts in the air. Following them is a throng of about forty men, women and children, Raramuri and mestizo. They're somber and prayerful, holding candles and rosaries. They're dedicated to honoring the path of the suffering Jesus and are guarded by a dozen soldiers carrying long, wooden spears.

After their loop through town is completed, they file into the church and place Jesus and Mary on the altar. As a diablo I'm not permitted inside the church, but I can hear the sounds of matracas, drums, and whistles vibrating and echoing within the walls of the sanctuary. Later, while the soldiers and Christians are in procession, I hear a man playing the violin from the belfry, quietly and so sweetly. On one loop I charge the steps with my gun and steal a glimpse of the altar alight with many candles and shrouded with the smoke of incense. The Virgin of Guadalupe is front center, flanked by Jesus and a host of saints wavering in candle shadow.

Late in the night while the diablos are raising a rowdy hell, the bearers of Jesus and Mary pass by the tesguino shed. One of the diablos rushes into the throng and grabs a soldier in a bear lock. The soldier tosses his spear to the ground. Quickly, the crowd spreads to give the two Raramuri men room to wrestle. I'd seen the Raramuri wrestle in Norigachi, but hadn't realized how skilled they are or how rough the matches are. I can barely see them through the cloud of dust in the dark night.

The woman who'd fashioned the GW Bush hat appears at my side and urges me to wrestle. I'm wobbly drunk so I actually consider the challenge. For a moment. Fortunately, I then have a moment of clarity. No, gracias. I don't dare. From what I'm seeing these men are very accomplished wrestlers with a lot of pride on the line. They have extraordinary strength and endurance and love wrestling as much as running and dancing.

How embarrassing for the gringo if a man half his size pins him to the ground, like my fellow diablo is doing to his opponent? I hear a loud thud as the soldier is slammed to the dirt. We throng the victor and race through town in celebration.

I have no idea of the time. The moon stands still over Guadalupe Coronado, refusing to budge an inch and allow the sun to rise. My legs are like rubber, the hardened paint pulls at my body hair, and my skin itches like crazy. The air is shivering cold. We haven't stopped since mid-morning yesterday, haven't slowed the pace, no food or water, and it has to be four in the morning, or later.

Three diablos are laid out on the ground in front of the tesguino shed. The jefe is unable to revive them, so he leaves them where they lie. I attempt to sit and rest, but two diablos quickly grab my arms and lift me to my feet. Only a few faithful remain from the crowd of onlookers, and they're staggering drunk. Many of the Raramuri women and children are huddled on the ground in the shadows at the edges of the village, sound asleep.

In a state of hilarity, dancing strong, yelping, drinking, we ridicule Judas Iscariot, calling him a drunkard and a crazy man, slapping his wooden phallus, pulling straws from his body. As the first hints of dawn spread through the canyon, I heft Papa Judas and carry him on my shoulders for a loop through the Stations of the Cross. I hadn't realized how heavy he is. I nearly stumble with the weight when I stoop beneath the pine-bough arches.

The GW Bush hat is still intact.

I'm still standing, almost to the finish line.

As our troupe passes through the arches, I recognize a fellow gringo who owns a hotel in the mountains. I can't say that I know him, but I'd met him on the trail a few times and in Urique at Plaza Restaurant. Caught up in the drama of the final acts of Semana Santa and fully inebriated, I challenge him to wrestle Raramuri-style. Doug and I are equal in age and size. He's a former Marine. I figure it's a fair contest.

He readily accepts.

We lock arms. The diablos circle around us, beside themselves with excitement. "Dos gringos luchando!"

They shout and pound the drums. "Luche! Luche!" Wrestle! Wrestle! We push and tug, looking for an advantage. I lose my feet, but quickly recover. I'm sobered by the exertion of strength. I have my hands full with a very strong man and much pride on the line in front of my brother diablos.

My legs are weakening. I have to make a move soon or he'll pin me to the ground, and I cannot let that happen.

We lock arms at the shoulders and shove with all our might, like two white bulls locking horns. I keep my eyes on his feet as I brace mine wider apart. When he slides his feet closer together, I turn him to the ground and pin his shoulders to the dirt.

Quickly I rise from the ground before he has a chance to recover, and run though the crowd, all the diablos thronging me, shouting and slapping my back like I'd won a gold medal at the Olympics!

As we pass in front of the church, two diablos hold their guns in front of them and charge up the steps. The women part to the sides and allow the men to enter the church. The rest of us follow behind their lead. Inside the sanctuary, our jefe instructs us to lie on the concrete floor. The floor is covered with a pool of cool water, an exquisite relief for my exhausted body.

The clicking matracas, drumbeats and shouts with ha ha ha's cease. No one speaks a word. Total silence prevails in the sanctuary. A holy spirit fills the ancient church. I have visions of Easters past—painted eggs, suits and ties, new dresses and shoes, congregants filling the churches, and a memory of preaching the resurrection of Christ from a pulpit. Now, I'm groveling on the floor of a simple church with a gang of devils, wobbly drunk on tesguino and weary from battling the Christians. And I conclude on the spot that I'd never been a part of a more sacred event. Holy devils on a mission.

At the word of the jefe, we scramble to our feet and rush out the door of the church. It's time for the grand finale of the ultramarathon event, the burning of Papa Judas. My traveling companions from North Carolina are among the crowd awaiting the dramatic climax. I see Allie frantically trying to get my attention and pointing at the effigy. The GW Bush hat is gone! We had waited all night to see the hat go up in flames.

Right before coming to the canyons, Allie and Bud had been arrested twice during the anti-war demonstrations in the streets of Asheville and were thrown in jail, where they were mocked and ridiculed for their lack of patriotism. The hat has great significance for them.

I spot the Raramuri woman who had made the hat, standing at the back of the crowd. She's holding the hat in her hand! Allie very politely asks her for the hat. She doesn't budge. Then Allie, with animated gestures, tries to explain how much we want the hat to burn with Judas. Still, she refuses. Bud wears a leather cap that had been the envy of many of the locals we'd met, so he offers it to the woman in trade—hat for hat. She ignores their entreaties and walks away with the GW Bush hat firmly in hand.

Judas Iscariot is set to fire. Diablos race through the courtyard twirling matracas. The entire throng is shouting and laughing and stumbling into each other. Three drummers bang the drums with wild abandon. As the flames rise closer and closer to Judas's head, the Raramuri woman pushes to the front of the mob and places the hat on the head of the effigy! Straw grass, sticks, a wooden phallus, and the GW Bush hat are engulfed with flames. The great betrayer is destroyed in Guadalupe Coronado.

"A banarse! A banarse, gringo!"

I'm not sure what they mean.

Three diablos excitedly pull me to the edge of the bluff and point to the river. Several of the diablos are already splashing in the water. As we descend the trail to the riverbank, my eyes are flooded with tears from my overwhelming sense of gratitude . . . and relief that I'd lasted the course. I'm awestruck by the sweetness of the Raramuri spirit, their childlike exuberance for life. Living in the harshest land they could find to preserve their rich culture, with only the crudest of material possessions. I conclude that they are wealthy beyond measure.

We dive into the cool, refreshing water again and again. Our masks slowly dissolve into the Urique. My white skin and their brown skin reappear. We're subdued and quiet, hearing only the drone of the river. The deerskin drums are silent, and the clicking matracas, the hypnotic beats of guitars, fiddles, flutes, hysterical Raramuri hoots ... all laid to rest until the next festival.

We wade to the riverbank and rest in the hot sun. Working together as we'd done from the beginning, we wash the paint from each other's backs, the scrubbing like a massage for exhausted muscles. Our jefe had kept us moving in tandem from start to finish. Todos con juntos. When a diablo strayed from the dance, the jefes herded him back to the flock like a wayward goat. When a diablo buckled to the ground from the potent tesguino, the jefes rushed to prod him to his feet. Early in the night, one of our gang broke his forearm in a wrestling match yet refused to bow out, and he endured to the end.

The strong hands on my back are heartfelt and generous. Brilliant sunlight accentuates the childlike essence shining in our faces.

The roly-poly man scampers towards the riverbank, toting our belongings in the feed sack. He neatly spreads the clothes across the rocks, fulfilling his appointed duty.

I hear a feeble whoop and ha ha ha. The final pronouncement. The curtain is drawn. My companions climb the rocky trail along the edge of the bluff to rejoin their friends and families. When the last of the tesguino is drained from the ollas, they will begin the arduous climb to their homes in the cliffs high above Guadalupe Coronado.

With splotches of black paint still staining my body I walk to Urique, about six miles downriver, tired to the bone, yet blessed like I'd been touched by all of creation.

CHAPTER ELEVEN

Solo Journeys

As soon as the morning Water Authority meeting is adjourned, I leave Asheville City Hall and decide to walk to The Summit, a name I gave to a camp spot on the Mountains-to-Sea Trail just off the Blue Ridge Parkway. I plan to take the city bus to a stop about 100 yards from the trail. That way I won't have to walk on the side of a busy street where there aren't any sidewalks.

After a full week of contentious meetings over air pollution, water, the city budget, and a "Reclaim the Streets" demonstration, my energy is drained—plus arthritis pain has worn me down. For the past week I've only been able to attend the meetings. The rest of the time I've stayed hidden in the woods, nursing my wounds. I need a long walk and few days of wilderness solitude to refresh.

I'm ready for communion with the wild, where all living things flow in their natural order.

Before leaving town, I hang out at Pack Square with Snakehawke and Flute John, trying to convince them to make the trek to The Summit. John claims he's given up long-distance walking since he hiked with Dave from Asheville to the Outer Banks, and Snakehawke's arthritic knees are no good on the trails.

John entertains us with a new ballad he's written for his flute. We keep an eye out for the cops, who are actively enforcing the new ordinance that requires a permit for playing a musical instrument in downtown—and with that, only in designated areas. Snakehawke and I agree to guard our outlaw brother.

"Did you get a permit to play music, John?"

"Hell, no."

I ask him if he ever paid that ticket from Rattlesnake Lodge when the Park Rangers stormed our camp.

"Hell, no. Did you?"

"No, I didn't pay it and never will. I think Dave and Mike did, though."

"Idiots."

I notice Snakehawke is wearing my old sandals, now wrapped in duct tape to keep the straps secured. When I walked back to Asheville from Virginia on the Blue Ridge Parkway, I wore a pair of flip-flops tied together with scrap pieces of string and padded with mullein leaves. By the time I reached the center of town they fell apart completely, leaving me barefoot with no means to buy another pair.

Fortunately, I ran into an old friend from high school—the same friend who had helped finance my trip to Honduras. He escorted me to a shoe store and gifted me with a new pair of sandals. A year later, the same friend bought me another pair of sandals. The clerk put the year-old pair in the shoebox. Just as I was walking out of the store, Snakehawke was coming towards me on the sidewalk. In perfect synchronicity I handed him the old sandals, and he's been wearing them ever since.

"Snakehawke, I bet those sandals have 10,000 miles on them by now."

"Yeah, and I bet they're good for another 10,000."

The autumn forest glows amber in the setting sun. Heeding their ancient instincts, the chattering squirrels scamper through crispy leaves beneath the twisted laurel, foraging for winter supplies. Droppings of fresh bear scat are scattered around the old fire pit, a sure sign that they also feel the nip in the air and are planning ahead for winter hibernation.

Gentle breezes sweep through the trees like whispers from a sacred spirit. Green and crimson maple leaves splashed with specks of gold swirl around me. Broad, yellow and rusty leaves of oaks and poplars snap from their twigs and dart to the ground, sounding like footsteps as they fall to the forest floor. At night I listen attentively to distinguish the sounds of the falling leaves from approaching bears, coyotes, or wayward humans.

A loud, swooshing sound jostles me from my reverie. A red-tailed hawk with a wingspan wider than my outstretched arms swoops into the thicket of trees. I've never seen one this large. For a few brief moments he perches on the limb of an oak tree right in front of me, staring into my eyes before flexing his wings and vanishing over the side of the mountain as mysteriously as he'd appeared.

The vision of the hawk, the guardian of the air, the harbinger of important messages. I sit still and consider the thoughts that come to mind in the wake of his appearance.

Air.

Only a few weeks ago I stood beside the Blue Ridge Parkway, watching an endless stream of SUVs, RVs, cars, and trucks zoom by—presumably carrying tourists viewing the same smog-laden valley through tinted windshields. While the sun dazzled the Carolina-blue skies, a brown-tinged blanket of smog pervaded the entire Asheville basin, obscuring the surrounding mountains.

The sharp juxtaposition of pristine woods and ugly, putrescent air jarred my sensibilities. When I reached town, my eyes burned and my throat grew raspy from the vapors. Then I saw clearly the toxic plague stealthily cooking the life from all the living beings in our mountains, particularly in the summer and fall when thousands and thousands of tourists converge on western North Carolina.

In town, I called the director of the local Air Quality Agency, who explained to me that what the media was calling haze during the unseasonably hot weather at the peak of leaf season was due to a lingering high-pressure system and a lack of wind and rain. The stagnant air traps the sulfates and nitrates from coal-fired power plants and automobile exhausts (now augmented by the seasonal influx of tourists) in the inhabited valleys.

He added that, under these conditions, "We cook in our own soup, so to speak."

Water.

The water issue in Asheville has been very taxing. After nearly famishing from dehydration in the Copper Canyons on several occasions, I've learned the critical place of water in our daily lives and I bring that urgency to the meetings, yet little if any progress is made.

Sadly, we've grossly polluted and foolishly wasted much of our water to the point that most people now use filters and drink bottled water to ensure their safety. Meanwhile, the infrastructure we've erected to deliver our drinking water is crumbling, despoiled by decades of neglect, political abuse, turf battles, lawsuits, threats of lawsuits and pork-barrel priorities. Water systems across the nation arc in a state of crisis, with little immediate hope of improvement.

In the creation accounts of most civilizations, water is the womb from which all life is birthed—as in the Book of Genesis where, in the opening act of creation, Elohim is seen brooding over the waters of the deep. Every mammal ever conceived was incubated in the nurturing fluid of the mother's womb and delivered into the world by its natural flow. Water is the principal constituent of all living organisms. It accounts for over sixty percent of human body weight.

Water is the cornerstone of religious ritual worldwide, symbolizing purification, consecration, and the unfathomable mysteries of life. In the ancient Greek Bible, the term for spiritual understanding and enlightenment is sunesis, which refers to the point where two rivers converge—like the Tigris and Euphrates in Mesopotamia, or the French Broad and the Swannanoa in Asheville. Whether it's the sacred ritual of baptism or the traditions of hand and foot washing or the divine experience of diving from the face of a boulder into a deep green pool on a hot summer day, it's clear that water is the life-sustaining power of creation.

We are water.

Consider the root meaning of amartia, the Greek Bible's word for sin, which symbolizes a canal of water that is clouded with mud and muck.

Pristine water, turbid politics.

The next day I make the long ascent to Rattlesnake Lodge, remembering the solo journey I'd made through the Urique Canyon and over the mountains to Batopilas. The rugged Blue Ridge Mountains aren't so dissimilar from the formidable mountains of the Sierra Madre. On the trails in both locations I sense the immensity of life and the latent power of creation. The land is intimate and comforting to the human mind, yet when I'm alone in the remote parts of the wilderness I'm often overwhelmed by the aloofness of the great Mother, keenly aware that she could destroy me in an instant without a shred of remorse. Especially when I'm alone.

In Mexico, I walked from Cerocahui in the sierra down the sides of the cliffs and through the Mescalerita gorge until I reached the town of Urique—a twelve-hour hike. I rested for a day in Urique and then continued down-river to Lalaha, where I crossed through the river and began the ascent into the cliffs on a trail not far from the path Susie and I had taken when we first descended into the Urique Canyon.

Like the time with Susie, I lost the trail I had intended to take and veered far to the southwest, farther and farther from my destination of Batopilas. I'd become familiar with the general directions of the Sierra Madre, so I didn't panic. I'd learned that losing my intended trail often leads me to unexpected discoveries—on the literal trail and in the regular flow of life experience.

As I rested beside a stream cascading through the heart of the mountain, a Raramuri man and his wife happened along the trail and stopped to speak to me. The man carried a sack of flour on his back. The tiny woman toted two handbags filled with groceries, and a baby that was tied to her back with a blanket. I was tired and sweaty from the steep ascent. They'd come the same distance and showed no signs of stress. For them the trail is simply the path to their home, the same path they'd scaled since birth, since they were tied to their own mothers' backs.

They invited me to follow them to their little adobe hut perched on the edge of the cliff, one among six other huts, all Raramuri. Thrilled by their offer of hospitality, I stayed for the night and helped them set a fire to cook supper. We talked late into the night under crystal-clear skies alive with shooting stars.

"Are you content to live so far removed from the rest of the world?"

The man searched my eyes like he was wondering why I would ask such an obvious question.

"Si, soy muy contento. Es la tierra de me familia por muchos anos." His wife nodded her head in agreement. She too had lived in the same place all her life, as had her ancestors as far back as anyone in the family can remember.

When it was time to sleep, they hauled a set of rusted box springs from inside the hut, covered the springs with handwoven blankets, and lay down for the evening. I heard husband and wife talking and giggling until late in the night. I listened, unable to decipher their words but blessed by the sweetness of their voices and the intimacy they conveyed. When they prepared our meal, husband and wife worked in tandem, equals in all familial affairs, as is the manner among all the Raramuri I'd met. In fact, I'd learned that the women are equal in all decision-making and always hold the deeds of property in their own names.

By the time I reach the springs at Rattlesnake Lodge, my shirt and pants are soaked with sweat. The heat in town is stifling and only a little cooler at 4,000 feet. My first choice is to camp in the usual spot close to the water, but during summer many people take day hikes to the springs, so I opt for the upper camp higher in the cliffs. There's no trail and the slope is steep. I bushwhack through the dense undergrowth, making wide detours and zigzags to avoid dense briar thickets.

I toss sticks and stones to warn the rattlesnakes of my approach. The place isn't called Rattlesnake Lodge for nothing. I don't encounter any snakes at all; nevertheless, I imagine them nesting among the rocks and slithering through the underbrush. When I reach the crest of the ridge, I enter the domain of the giant stinging nettle that dominates the top of the ridge—a forest of stalks growing as high as my chest. I raise my bare arms above the prickles, cautiously sliding through the thicket until I reach the campsite.

A few long strips of bark that I used for siding have fallen to the ground, but otherwise the lean-to I constructed several years ago is still intact. The stack of firewood from my last trip is just as I left it. My old cook pot hangs from the front corner of the hut. There are no signs of others having ventured upon the camp—except for bears. Piles of scat lie near the fire pit. I'm certain it's bear crap, no more than a day old.

I set up camp, taking care not to brush against the stinging nettle. Even though the heat at midday is stifling, I light a fire to smudge the hordes of gnats and mosquitoes swarming my face and hands. I hang my wet clothes in the sun to dry. I don't have extra clothing, so I sit naked in a cloud of smoke to cleanse the side effects of urban living from my body and soul. The ever-present threat of bears, rattlesnakes, swarms of bloodsucking bugs, stinging nettle, with no trail to the top of the ridge, should insure my privacy.

I cook a pot of beans with garlic, onions, salt, and pepper, adding leaves of stinging nettle—the tender shoots from the bottom of the stalks. The raw, earthy leaf is potent food for the body and mind. By the time I'm done with my meal, the sun has set and refreshing breezes sweep through the forest. I pull on my clothes and settle in for a night of solitude with the animate wilderness.

That time I made my first solo journey through the canyons, I'd imagined a night of solitude in the wild after I left the home of the Raramuri couple. My new friend, Arnulfo, had drawn a map in the dirt describing the trails to follow from his hut to the town of Batopilas. He claimed that I should make it to the other canyon by nightfall. Late in the afternoon when the sun was easing towards the horizon, I was still crossing the peaks through the rocky spires far above the Urique River, still the most part of a day from Batopilas.

I'd never felt more overwhelmingly alone in all my life. The silence was so pronounced it seemed like I was engulfed by an enormous presence. The clouds were twisted in uncanny shapes, and the sky was a kaleidoscope of colors. I kept my eyes riveted to the trail to calm the dizziness swimming in my head. By the time I reached the very top where the trail leveled for a stretch, I began searching for a good spot to camp for the night and rest my weary legs. I'd climbed all day with very few respites on the rock-filled trail.

In retrospect, while sitting beside my fire above Rattlesnake Lodge, I view that experience as my truest initiation into the wilderness. I'd faced all the fears that crop up when alone in the wild, heightened by the reality that I was in a foreign country in some of the most redoubtable land in the world, where survival is no guarantee. I knew that if I hurt myself or fell from the cliffs, my body would probably never be recovered. At times images of my death arose into my mind unsolicited. I could vividly picture myself sliding off the mountain and splattering across the boulders at the bottom of the canyon.

The rising flames of my campfire cast an ethereal glow across the meadow of green nettle and mayflowers and illuminate the trunks of the massive trees. Silhouettes of dead trees lean against the living ones, life and death interpenetrated, and the ones half-rotted on the ground supply sustenance to untold species of burgeoning life. The electric buzz of a million cicadas and crickets suffuses the wilderness. I sense the proximity of black bears and coyotes and rattlesnakes.

The presences of the living woods expose my egotisms. The clear light of the vital fire pierces my illusions of self-deception and consumes the false gods that bedim my vision. My blood whispers to me from the ancient of days. Now, nothing stands between my heart and the heart of the palpable earth. I sing quietly with the voice of my soul in the temple of the living and the dying.

I imagine my death, my body rotting beneath the dirt like the trees in their holy cemetery. I see the worms and maggots, flies and gnats, vultures and four-legged beasts feasting upon my body. What was once a nightmare of horrors upon horrors is a sober reality. Rot and new birth interwoven. No more fantasies of angels and streets paved with gold; only the loamy dirt and life at the root of existence.

I remember reading an entry from my college journals about preaching a revival at which I organized a Burn the Chaff Day with the teenagers. We built a bonfire in a field beside the church cemetery, and the young people brought everything they believed hindered their witness for the Lord. I spoke about the coming of Christ and the consequences of being left behind on earth and facing the tribulation.

We burned hundreds of record albums, eight-track tapes, Ouija boards, jewelry, trinkets, pictures, clothes, etc. The rock-and-roll music of Satan went up in flames, the smoke like a sweet offering to the Lord. The Rolling Stones, Janis Joplin, The Beatles, Bob Dylan, The Doors would no longer poison the minds of these young people. One of the football players burned a box full of Playboy magazines. We all cried and held hands and sang songs of praise to almighty God.

Little did I know then that over thirty years later I'd finally have the strength to carry my own chaff to the burning ground, including the religious idols I'd so zealously upheld in my sermon at that revival.

Since my teenage years as an aspiring evangelist, I've awakened from a long nightmare of depression and despair and religious torment. I have climbed from the bottom of a deep ravine to the open light. Only in the wilderness have I found the insight to deprogram my fundamentalist indoctrination and maintain the power to break the curse of bipolar disorder. Walking long distances for months at a stretch has provided time to observe the dynamics of my cycles and to accept them as teachers and not as a threat to be feared.

In the solitude of the camp, I hear my blood pleading for me to accept myself as I am and to view my highs and lows not as a disease, but as teachers who instruct me in the ways of the silence, the movement, and the rest. Slowly, I've gained strength.

The way of the path, literal and figurative, reveals itself step-by-step, requiring trust in the presence of the moment and, from that center, all things fall in place in a good and timely way for all concerned. So much of the great prose and poetry of the ascetics, the wanderers and seekers who have traveled by foot and lived with the earth, alludes to the intimate companion on the wilderness path. I still hold many of the religious icons who have graced the world's history in high esteem, but I've begun to develop my own identity, dream my own metaphors, and canonize my own collection of sacred writ.

Through my relationships with the people of the Copper Canyon, I've grown to believe that soundness of mind and body is directly related to one's proximity to dirt, rocks, trees, flowers, and birds.

The Raramuri have invigorated my faith by teaching me by example to be a genuine human being with my feet deeply planted in the earth. In my presence, they've never discussed Christianity or attempted to persuade me to follow any particular path. No, for me, the spirituality of the Raramuri lies in their naturalness. They are spiritual because they are of the earth, present with themselves and their habitat.

Before, I awoke each morning in my private box, walked out the door and down the concrete sidewalk to my mobile box. I drove my mobile box into town and parked in a giant box for mobile boxes, and then walked across concrete and asphalt paths to my office box, where I typed on computer boxes until I lay down on the couch in the evening to watch the TV box. On Sundays I even worshipped in a church box.

In my past I would go days, even weeks without natural light, without touching the earth or breathing fresh air. Is it any wonder I grew so alienated from any semblance of creative living? Is it such a shock that my brain had nowhere to go except into locked patterns of mania and depression?

In contrast to my former urban-box life, I recall a moment in the canyons when Susie and I were camped beside the Urique River.

The sound of splashing water awakened me.

Three Raramuri teenagers arose from the river like amphibians from another age. Their sleek young bodies glistened with sunlight and dripping water, and their thick black hair matted to their heads. Barefoot and wearing loincloths—a vision of cave dwellers, of primitives untainted by the modern world, preserved in their pristine naturalness.

They scaled the side of a boulder set at the edge of the river and crawled across the top, disappearing on the other side. We heard talking and giggling and then splashing, like they were diving into the water from the rock.

Slowly, I walked towards the boulder. The boys withdrew into shyness when they realized my presence. I stepped through a side creek and stood across the pool from where they'd perched on the side of the rock. Two large fish flapped on the rocks near where I stood.

At first I was puzzled. The common fishing gear in the canyons is a hook with string wrapped around a stick or a beer can, but they apparently didn't have any kind of gear. The only other possibility was that they had caught the fish with their hands! They wouldn't make eye contact, so I called to ask if they had caught the fish. They shyly nodded yes and demonstrated that they had caught them with their hands, con mano.

I asked them if they would catch two more fish. "I'll pay you for your work," I promised. I acted out my Spanish words, holding my arms like I was diving into the water and grabbing a fish with my hands. They held their hands across their mouths and giggled at my antics. Suddenly, one of the guys dived into the pool while the other two watched him. The boy stayed underwater far longer than I could hold my breath, probably longer than most who aren't water people.

Finally he broke the surface, smiling broadly, with a three- to four-pound fish squirming in his hands. He tossed the fish to the rocks near the others. Not to be outdone, one of his companions dived from the rock and hauled another fish to the bank, much more quickly.

They sat perched on the boulder looking my way, obviously content with their world-class performance for delighted gringos. I dived into the pool and swam to the edge of the boulder with 100 pesos for the fish. They took the money and disappeared over the boulder as suddenly as they had appeared. Susie and I constructed a crude rock oven and cooked the fish atop a smooth stone, basting the fish with oil drained from a can of sardines. We added a little salt and enjoyed one of the most memorable feasts of our lives.

As I lie down to sleep at my camp above Rattlesnake Lodge I wonder if the bear will venture into my camp in the wee hours of the night, or if a lonely rattler will crawl into my sleeping bag for warmth from the chilly air. I comfort myself with visions of dancing diablos.

Early the next morning I hike down the side of the mountain to replenish my water supply at the springs. The cool air is sweet to my body. I walk slowly and deliberately through the brush, at peace and grateful for profound sleep and great gulps of woodsy air. Images of coiled rattlesnakes keep my eyes riveted to the ground as I thread my way through the rocks and fallen trees.

Suddenly, I hear the leaves shaking vigorously at the crown of a long, tall tulip poplar growing straight as an arrow about fifteen yards from where I stand. I shield my eyes from the glare of the light, expecting a giant red-tailed hawk to emerge from the canopy of dense foliage and soar into the air, as I'd witnessed at The Summit. I freeze dead in my tracks, breathless. The entire upper half of the tree is shaking with a commotion that I'm sure could not be made by a hawk, no matter how large.

In another split second, a large black bear appears from the thick bush of limbs.

Head first, he runs down the trunk of the tree. Head first! He's moving so fast he's a black blur in my vision. I can hear the clatter of his claws digging into the bark and his feral grunts of exertion. As soon as he hits the ground, he tears through the underbrush as quick and nimble as a squirrel and disappears down the side of the mountain out of my sight.

I sit on the ground beneath the tree, grasping for comprehension of what I'd just witnessed. My hands are shaking. Adrenalin is in my throat. For a split second, I'd thought he was coming for me. I'm only a few yards from the base of the tree. I would've been dead before I knew what had happened to me. Then it dawned on me that I had startled him and that he was running in fear. He was afraid of me! How ironic! I'm astonished by his power and strength. To be able to run vertical to the ground carrying 400 or 500 pounds is unimaginable. I wouldn't have believed it if I hadn't seen it with my own eyes.

For the remainder of the day I sit by the fire, my skin tingling from the virile potency of the wild bear.

The next week I hike alone into the heart of Pisgah mountain along Yellow Dog Creek and camp in a patch of giant ferns. I awake from an afternoon nap to the thunder of a dozen giant pileated woodpeckers pounding a stand of dead trees. The cacophonous sounds rock my gypsy soul.

Chapter Twelve

Ya Cumpli! Ya Cumpli!

Late in the night, two soldiers rush into our dance circle and clasp my arms, hustling me inside the church, through the crowded sanctuary, all the way to the altar.

The smoke of pine incense billows to the ceiling of the ancient sanctuary. Flaming candles cast a mystical glow over the portrait of the Lady of Guadalupe and the host of saints flanking her on each side. Clicking matracas, shouts, whistles, and drums reverberate inside the walls. In the shadows, the prayerful chords of a violin. The effigy of Jesus lying in the coffin appears so real I shiver.

The soldiers motion for me to carry the coffin. As a diablo I'm obligated to serve as they direct, so I heft the wooden support beams to my shoulders, straining under the weight, quickly shifting my feet for balance. A fellow diablo holds up the front beams and we carry the casket through the sanctuary, down the steps of the church, and begin another procession through the Stations of the Cross.

I'm nearly a foot taller than my companero, so I'm forced to flex my knees for levity as we halt and resume our journey again and again for an hour. My only cue is the feet of the diablo in front. I breathe deeply so that I keep my attention totally riveted to my current task. I can't stumble or lose my strength, no small task since we have already danced for many hours and have drunk copious amounts of tesguino. I'm aware that we are actors in a primitive passion play, yet each of us is completely absorbed in our part, as if we've transformed into the personalities we represent.

As we return the coffin to the altar, I imagine living in Spain in the seventeenth century and serving as a young Jesuit, zealous to carry the passion of Jesus to the dark corners of the Sierra Madre mountains of Mexico. By the time I was twenty, I'd already preached the fundamentalist Christian message from pulpits all over the USA. I had studied ancient Greek for five years, parsed the scriptures of the old manuscripts from Genesis to Revelations, committed whole books of the New Testament to memory, and prayed on my knees until they were worn raw.

I'm sure I would have answered the call for high adventure in a mysterious land to endure hardship for the Lord and evangelize the savages and heathens for the cross and the crown. I'd preached my own brand of Jesuit heaven and hell, sin and guilt, shame and eternal damnation. Like the idol of my past, the Reverend Billy Graham, I had pounded the pulpit and admonished thousands to receive the new birth in Jesus Christ or risk eternity in the fire of a devil's hell.

If I'd come to the ancestors of these same Raramuri people, would I have condemned their ancient ceremonies or instead danced with them in their "pagan" rituals?

How many Jesuits went native and stayed in these canyons until Spain dimmed in their memory and the doctrine of hell vanished from their vocabulary, I muse. Did any see the folly of their patriarchy and their angry god while dwelling with gentle Raramuri souls, many of whom live naturally in the balance of sun and moon?

Was there a young Jesuit with a vision of Jesus dancing and drinking tesguino among the diablos?

As the women throng the altar, chanting prayers, waving incense over the coffin, I see clearly there is no separation between life and myth. The Raramuri are Jesus, the Virgin of Guadalupe, el Diablo, tesguino, the earth of the canyons, the fire and sun and moon.

The soldiers halt my attempt to exit and direct me to a miniature thatched hut in the back of the church. Inside is an offering of corn, squash, and beans spread over a blanket at the foot of a statue of the Virgin Mary. They hand me a wooden spear and order me to stand guard in front of Mary.

I stand very still and erect while my thoughts drift to memories of the first year I served. Then, I was propelled by sheer adrenalin for the entire thirty-some hours of dancing and running with the diablos. I was so completely caught by surprise that I had been invited to participate that I didn't even consider the stringent physical demands that would be required. I found the strength to stay the course and make it to the finish line without passing out. When I dived into the Urique River, I was keenly aware that I'd satisfied lifelong desires to experience life at the most rudimentary level, like I had connected with long-neglected strands of my genetic code.

The second year, to reach the designated grounds of the paint ceremony, we climbed into the cliffs for over three hours when the temperatures hovered around 110 degrees, and had to return the same distance just to commence the ceremony. As we reached the pueblo, I had spotted Stephanie, my daughter, swimming in the river with some of her Raramuri friends. I held her image in my mind as I struggled through that night. After Judas was burned, I hobbled to the river, completely depleted of energy and very grateful that I had somehow managed to successfully complete another year.

In my third year, I savor every minute of the long ritual.

We dance and dance under the three-quarter moon, sprint through the Stations of the Cross on every loop, drink gallons of tesguino, and wrestle like madmen with the soldiers. Again and again the soldiers order us to carry the heavy cross and the coffin of Jesus and stand guard over Mary, and we take turns shouldering the burdensome effigy of Judas Iscariot.

"I've been born again among the Raramuri in the land of the Great Mother," I whisper. And shout, "whoop whoop whoop, ha ha ha!" Fellow diablos laugh at my exuberance, yet have no idea of my history or what I'm feeling at the moment.

How ironic to say so; how unlikely; how long in coming. They'd helped transport me from the illusions of my religious deities and placed my feet on the living earth. With their simple way of life as an example, I have very clearly discerned the fallacies inherent in a culture based on consumerism. Most importantly the Raramuri have inspired me to rise above my physical and mental ailments.

As soon as I'm relieved of my duties in the church I return to the tesguino shed, gulp down a cup, and take my place in the dance line.

The first and second year, I arrived in Guadalupe Coronado for Semana Santa the day before the commencement of the ceremony, so I'd had only a peripheral understanding of the work involved in preparations. This year I arrived a month early. The first days we cleared weeds with machetes around Arroyo Hondo, which would later serve as the dressing room for the diablos; pitched rocks from the trail so the diablos would have smooth sailing when we dashed into Guadalupe to commence the ceremony; made repairs on the little adobe hut; and built standing metates to grind corn for tesguino.

For two days I assisted Fernando and Chico, our designated jefes, chopping and hauling firewood. They cut small trees with machetes and axes, trimmed the branches, and slid the logs down the sides of the hills, while another diablo and I carried them on our shoulders to the camp. We'd kept motivated to continue laboring in the sweltering sun, knowing our efforts would help supply gallons of corn beer for the duration of the dance.

For the first time in my three-year experience, I drank tesquino made by the sweat and toil of my own labor.

One day a group of eight diablos gathered in town to put a new roof on the community building behind the church, which would later serve as diablo headquarters during the ceremony. As is often their custom, we waited until the heat of the early afternoon to commence the most difficult part of our day's work. With sweat flooding my bald head, I asked Chico why we'd waited for the hottest part of the day. Chico just smiled, and then directed another diablo and me to carry two large ollas to Arroyo Hondo as soon as we'd finished the roof.

We did as he directed, without argument. The ollas weigh fifty pounds or more and the walk to the camp is about thirty minutes from town, uphill. We lifted about twenty more five-gallon buckets filled with dirt and spread it over the roof. As soon as the roof was done, we hefted the ollas to our shoulders and headed up the mountain on the shadeless trail.

On the third day of our operation in Arroyo Hondo, Irene appeared to help supervise the work camp. Along with her were Marie Elena and her little son. Irene is an older woman, maybe sixty years old. I guess. She could be forty or eighty. She moves her lanky body with ease and dignity, never in a rush yet always busy from early in the morning until late in the evening. Tall and lean with smooth, deep-brown skin, she fidgeted with her red scarf like she wanted to hide more of her face from me.

She had as yet to decide who I am and why I'd been chosen to participate in the workforce. I attempted to have a conversation with her, only to have her ignore me like I didn't even exist—like so many others. Even Chico questioned her timidity with me. She just shook her head and giggled.

When asked his age, Sebastian counts each of his ten fingers and then turns nine fingers down, which most interpret to mean he's ninety years old. No one knows, but they say that's close. One evening near dusk he appeared in camp standing beside a bush aflame with purple flowers, enjoying the sweet aromas. I hadn't heard him enter the grounds of the camp. He sat with me by the fire and claimed he'd walked eight hours from the tops of the mountains.

He graciously accepted a cup of coffee and told me his knees were tired, and laughed about how he's no longer able to walk the canyons like he'd once done. Sebastian speaks with a high-pitched, effeminate voice that at times changes to a deep-throated bass. When he speaks Raramuri with Irene, his singsong voice is mesmerizing. Ninety years old, walked eight hours on precarious mountain trails, and his only complaint was tired knees. Not a spot of sweat on him, no dust, fresh face aglow. With Sebastian I had the sense he could appear and disappear at will.

He is reputed to be a master tesguino maker among the Raramuri of Urique canyon, and a shaman who's very adept at healing with natural herbs and is known to be a faithful prayer warrior.

He has herded goats all of his life, he told me. So, in hopes of establishing common ground with him and to let him know that I'd been in his homeland many times, I tell him a story about a goat that was gifted to me a few years back.

I was camped in the Mescalera gorge at the home of Angel and Anita Bautiste. Sebastian knows them and Mescalera very well.

Anita casually made her way down the hill above our camp leading a goat by a rope. She tied the rope to a tree so that the goat's feet barely touched the ground. Then, she left the goat and crawled through the arroyo to her home on the other side.

Just before dawn the cries of the goat awakened me. I couldn't believe it was still tied to the tree. The poor goat was wailing with despair and exhaustion.

As soon as dawn light filled the Mescalera canyon, one of the Bautiste boys climbed through the arroyo and asked to borrow my hunting knife. I obliged him, but remained perplexed. They have plenty of knives. Knives are essential to their existence. Why did they want to borrow mine? And he took the goat with him.

The mystery was solved as soon as I heard the unmistakable cry of a desperate goat whose throat was being slit. I crawled out of my sleeping bag and made my way through the arroyo to the Bautistes' house.

One of the boys clutched the goat's head with two hands while Anita held a wooden bowl under its throat, collecting the blood spurting from the gash. They dressed the goat with great care and hung the parts over tree branches while blood spattered the dust. Within an hour Anita served me a plate of goat meat, the heart, the liver and the intestines, garnished with garlic and onions. She tossed a stack of hot tortillas on the table and motioned for me to eat.

Anita was obviously proud of her work, so I pretended to be pleased. The heart of the goat was well fried, but I couldn't escape the image of it still beating where it lay on my plate. I deeply appreciated her gesture of honor to her guests, but I could barely choke down the meal.

Sebastian beamed, agreeing with me that it was a gesture of honor and genuine hospitality.

Irene and Sebastian arose from their blankets at first light and began preparing breakfast of tortillas, beans, and squash with chilis and onions. They worked through the day until the light disappeared into dusk. We waited five days for the corn kernels to sprout underneath damp bedsheets, and then together we ground corn, rinsed it, and kept the large tubs of water and corn mash churning with blazing fires. The heat was intense and the work demanding, but our camaraderie was a joy and we refreshed ourselves with grapefruits and guayaba growing fat on the trees nearby.

I'm astounded by their strength, even as elders.

I'd first witnessed the extraordinary physical prowess of Raramuri when Susie and I hiked down the Urique River on our way to Norigachi.

Near the old footbridge below Lalaha, we sat on our backpacks in the shade of three large mesquite trees. Soon a group of four Raramuri men and one woman appeared on the trail toting ten-foot rolls of lamina—sheet metal for roofing. They balanced the lamina on their shoulders on scraps of cardboard, laughing as they walked, not a drop of perspiration on their foreheads. They stopped and rested alongside us, all smiles, surprisingly not at all shy and aloof in our presence like most of the Raramuri we'd met.

They had come all the way from the center of Urique, about a three-hour walk for Susie and me. While they watched, I strained to lift one of the rolls of lamina as high as my knees. They had carried the lamina like a bag of feathers, including the woman who was less than five feet tall and a wisp of weight. I wasn't even certain if I could hoist the roll to my shoulder, and I'm no weakling. I didn't try.

After a few sips of river water they continued on their way, playful, without burden, like kids on their way home from school. We heard faint yelps from far down the canyon as they headed towards home and a new roof. Susie and I agreed to never again complain about the weight of our backpacks.

Recently, I'd been a firsthand witness to the ability of the Raramuri to run long distance. I'd read accounts of them running deer to exhaustion, yet I figured it was an exaggeration. When I saw the

Raramuri in the annual fifty-mile ultramarathon held in Urique, I was fully convinced of their strength and power.

I viewed the runners framed by sheer canyon walls, kicking dust along the rocky ledge above the Urique River. Arnulfo Quimare, the premier Raramuri runner from the mountains near pueblo Munerachi, passed our lookout point running like a mountain deer with coyotes nipping at his heels. I stood on the bluff along with twenty or more people thrilled by the spectacle, amazed by the speed of the frontrunners and the fierce determination in their eyes to complete the grueling race.

Some fifty runners hailing from the USA, Europe and Mexico, including young and old, men and women, brown-skinned and white, started the race in downtown Urique. The Raramuri runners dressed in traditional clothes—bright scarves and headbands that trailed to the middle of their backs, blouse tops, loincloths, and most notably their tire-tread sandals strapped to their ankles with strips of leather. The gringos sported the best track shoes money can buy and water sacs strapped to their backs and stashes of energy bars at the refreshment stations.

I knew I was viewing the purest moment of athleticism I'd ever witnessed during my lifetime of involvement in sports, as a participant and as a spectator. Hundreds of delighted fans cheered the racers throughout the course and thronged the lead runners as they crossed the finish line nearly seven hours later. Serenaded by the blaring horns of a mariachi band, the exhausted participants danced with jubilation and relief that the grueling challenge had been completed. In the evening the whole town and many from the pueblitos near Urique swarmed the town plaza to celebrate with music, dance, and beer.

"Tres anos!"

I dive into the cool, emerald waters of Rio Urique and emerge with my arms raised in the air like a victorious athlete at the finish line.

"Ya cumpli! Ya cumpli!"

I cup my hands to my mouth and shout, my jubilation echoing through the confines of the narrow canyon. I have completed my three-year commitment, still standing.

I can't believe my great fortune. I clasp Hermanisillo's hands and look into his eyes. "Thank you for allowing me to dance at Holy Week with your people," I yell in Spanish. "Que muy bueno!"

A smile lights his face as he quickly plunges into the water, too innately shy to openly accept my affection. The first times I was around him, he was polite, never poking fun at me like Alvaro and so many of the others. He remained aloof, his posture reminding me I was an intruder into the isolated culture of his Raramuri homeland. A chabochi, the bearded one, an outsider.

The day before the festivities for Semana Santa started, I gifted him a pack of new guitar strings I had brought from the States. He received my gift with delight, exuding the essence of a little boy in the strong body of a hardworking man. While serenading the diablos, he'd beamed with pride every time our eyes met, an encouraging sign that I'd finally been accepted among his people.

I'd worked on several projects in the community with him, and we'd served together for two years as diablos. Several times he'd observed me out of step with the dance and had patiently shown me the correct way—and made certain I never missed a round of tesguino. During the ceremony he had strummed his guitar all day and night, never resting, never showing signs of fatigue. The same simple riffs over and over. I was astounded by his endurance and that he—along with all the others—never showed strain in his face or his body when he exerted such great effort.

The diablos dive into the river again and again like desert wanderers who've finally come to the water. What an exquisite relief to cleanse the dust, sweat, and paint from my body! Finally the itching begins to subside. The cool water helps soothe my depleted muscles and heavy eyelids. I'm thoroughly exhausted, but my joy is barely containable.

Alone, I walk away from Guadalupe Coronado, along the banks of the Urique River. The shadow of a hawk glides along the trail and then swerves across the rippling water. I raise my head to follow the bird's flight, and I'm dizzied by the enormity of the mountains dwarfing my presence. The imposing boulders simmer in the scorching sun, cloaked in a haze of intense heat. A sudden burst of drumming echoes through the stone chasm. Like a natural reflex I step to the dance, but my legs are too heavy with fatigue.

I wade into the river to cool down and coax enough life into my calves and thighs to finish the six-mile walk into the town of Urique. I'm surprised I feel no side effects from drinking so much corn beer. "Puro maize," the proud Raramuri shouted. I've had plenty of hangovers in my life, but not from tesguino. Catalyzed by extreme physical exertion over a prolonged period of time, the tesguino grounded me in a state of lucid awareness.

The effect was like a hallucination. I have experienced hallucinations through psilocybin mushrooms and a few times with LSD, and without a doubt the experiences were profound; however, I felt very different with tesguino. Dancing in a trancelike state, I remained very present with my body, my thoughts, and my fellow diablos. Instead of traveling into faraway visions and phantasmagoric imagery, I felt as if I'd entered a state of ultimate reality, like the tesguino had seeped in and inspired ancient memories encoded in my DNA. The other activities transpiring through the night in Guadalupe seemed far removed from our inner circle.

I remember having clear images of Dave during the night, whistling his bamboo flute as we walked along the beaches of the Outer Banks in North Carolina. I felt a deep sense of gratitude for him, that he'd shown me the purifying essence of long-distance walking and that he had guided me into the intimacy of the wilderness, thus leading me into the intimacy of my own soul.

I'd been refreshed by Dave's enthusiasm for the simple things of life and his childlike delight in living each moment of the day, the same characteristics that have so inspired me with the Raramuri.

As the drums vibrated through my body, I'd experienced a very lucid remembrance of the time Dave and I went to camp behind the veil of the falls at Moore's Cove, to prepare for a journey to Honduras. We'd stacked piles of firewood in the corner of the cave-like recess and arranged our bedding on the dirt floor of a smooth, flat ledge. Above us the stream leapt across the sharp outcropping, roaring to the creek bed below.

Water song filled the cave. The cold air, little affected by brief periods of sunlight in the deep recesses of the cove, stitched a mosaic of icicles like tigers' teeth at the upper rim of the cave. As soon as our campfire was roaring, strong showers of snow burst from the skies, the giant flakes transforming the cove into a sea of pure white, the mouth of the cave like a picture window into a winter dreamscape.

Since childhood I'd gone to the cave and imagined the times when the Cherokee people gathered at the falls. I'd never researched books to verify that they lived in that very spot. No signs of cave art. No arrowheads or shards from clay pots. No, more certain were the whispers of their blood echoing in the cave late at night, and their songs of jubilation and sorrow flowing with the waterfall.

We camped behind the falls for two days. Friends from town found our camp, then more friends, and others that we met under the falls for the first time. When the temporary campers returned to town they left supplies of food and drink until the big, flat rock enclosing the ledge was set like a banquet table. Two days turned into two weeks. Two months later, still comfortably ensconced in our winter den, thoughts of a journey to Honduras faded.

One morning Dave looked across the fire and asked, "Where were we going?" His eyes danced with a little boy's sense of wonder and delight.

I laughed, "To Moore's Cove, I reckon."

Just walk out the door, Dave had shouted that night at Vincent's Ear, and I walked out the door, leaving my past behind, and found my way to the Sierra Raramuri and this moment in the sand beside the Urique River with diablo stains on my body, yet purified within as if by fire.

Then I had glimpses of Thomas Didymus and how Jesus is lucky to have him as a brother, and how the craziest man I'd ever met had helped me find my own sanity.

I arrive at the old footbridge that spans the river. I can see the first adobe homes at the edge of pueblo Urique, and others on around the bend. I seek shade beside the river before I attempt the final leg. I bury my feet in the cool sand and try to rub more life into my calves and shins. A burst of exhilaration tingles through me and pours out as laughter, like I had laughed so many times during the night, bowled over by the absurdities of life and fate and how I could have possibly arrived among these people living on the edge of civilization.

Now, I lift my feet from the sand and struggle into my backpack. I decide to bypass the walk bridge and wade across the Urique River to feel the rush of water on my skin one more time. I stand waist deep in the strong current, listening to the faint echo of a drumbeat. I smell achiote incense. The image of the Virgin de Guadalupe flickers in candlelight. Painted diablos dance up a cloud of dust.

Or is it my imagination? I don't know. It doesn't matter. I will hear and feel the drumbeats of the Raramuri as long as I live.

Epilogue

El Ojo de la Agua

At dawn we walk to the bathhouse to soak in the hot mineral water. Jake, my younger son, chooses a pool and latches the door behind him. I enter Room 4 because the pool is larger and allows me to stretch my long legs and arms. I place the wooden plug in the hole of the tiled pool, stopping the stream of water that surfaces from beneath the ground just outside the bathhouse. When I'm finished I'll remove the plug and the water will flow into the sequia or canal outside the building.

I stay submerged for about fifteen minutes and then sit on the bench to cool down. When I'm fully relaxed I slip into the pool again, over and over, throughout the day and night. The warm water penetrates to the core of my muscles and into the marrow of my arthritic joints. For the first time in months, I find relief from the aches and stiffness of arthritic pain. Smiles spread across my face with greater ease, and I enjoy real laughter with my son.

The water of the Urique River in the Copper Canyon of northern Mexico is sacred water, like the water at Rattlesnake Lodge in the Blue Ridge Mountains of North Carolina. They hold a place in my life like intimate companions from the roots of my existence. Yet the water that gushes from beneath the Chihuahuan desert and into this bathhouse is of another dimension. The local people in the little pueblo of San Diego de Alcala call the thermal springs El Ojo, which literally means eye in Spanish, but is commonly used in reference to a spring.

The eye into the essence of all that is life.

I meet Jake by the outdoor pool, where we sit in the shade under the thatched ramada. Clouds of steam rise from the water that flows through the sequias. The mountains that surround the vast plains of ocotillo, thorny shrubs, aloe, and mesquite are shrouded in blue haze. The green leaves of los alamos trees glisten along the banks of the Chuviscar River. Today, the temps will rise into the low 100's. Now, the cool morning breeze refreshes our bodies, still flushed from the heat of the baths.

Jake yelps like he often does when he's filled with excitement, and three grackles flush into the air with wild squawks. His contented smile tells me he's cherishing pain-free moments same as me. Jake has juvenile rheumatoid arthritis. At the age of sixteen, he's already well acquainted with pain. We commiserate in the rough times and acknowledge the limitations that arthritis places on our lives and bemoan all the lonely hours we spend in pain when we don't want others to know. Without words, we understand each other's appreciation for the curative power of the springs. Every morning Jake is up at first light, ready for his daily bath.

The first time I came to San Diego de Alcala, I thought I'd discovered the living waters of the Garden of Eden.

I was en route to the Copper Canyon, but I decided to visit a friend in Delicias, a small town about an hour's drive from Chihuahua City. Abundio noticed that I winced with pain when I climbed from the car or arose from a chair. He suggested that we spend a day at a remote place in the desert where water flows from hot, mineral-rich springs and contains healing powers.

"Las aguas son muy rico y muy curativo," he promised.

Abundio suggested we spend the afternoon in the water and afterwards he would take me to the bus station in Chihuahua City so I could resume making way to the Copper Çanyon.

Four months later, I was still in the water at San Diego de Alcala, all plans for the canyons cancelled.

The caretaker at El Ojo entrusted me with my own key to the bathhouse and a permanent camp spot within the grounds. The first three weeks I existed only for the water. At three a.m., when the coyotes awakened me, I soaked for an hour and set a fire and made tea and listened to the wild dogs. Brilliant starlight and moonlight glowed over the desert. At sunrise and sunset I sat in a state of grace and mercy. My mind rested in peace.

I was often enveloped by a numinous presence that filled every part of me. The little window above the pila in the baths was like a portal through which I could clearly distinguish the fine line between illusion and reality.

I shared these things with Jake, and he understood. Those who suffer pain from an early age bear a deep wisdom.

"What does numinous mean?" Jake asked.

"Numinous means mystical or spiritual, but the word presence is sufficient for me. At different times in my life I've called the presence God, Jesus, the Holy Spirit, the Great Mother, the All in All, the Universe, and various other names. Yet there really isn't an adequate word. We know of a presence when we step into the water, don't we? Here, in this desert, in the sun and moonlight.

"I see the presence in my son and my son sees the presence in me. When I'm able to experience the intimacy of life as I do in the pools, I'm restored to the center of my being. Period. I no longer need a religious name or a book of scriptures or a church to legitimize the experience, as I did for so many years. That's about all I care to say in words."

"Amen, Dad."

My daughter Stephanie and I have spent so much time together in the wild that camping on the grounds of the springs with steam baths is like a vacation at a five-star resort. When people ask her about trips to the Copper Canyon with her Dad, she says, "Well, it's no vacation."

By all appearances, San Diego de Alcala is no vacation hot spot either. The last twenty miles on the rutted dirt road are slow, rough going, and hard on a car. There are no restaurants in town and only two small tiendas. The official population is eighty people, but sometimes you drive through town and don't see anyone.

The sun is fierce, shade is limited, and furious sandstorms are a way of life. Yet hidden in a craterlike dip about two miles from town sits a rustic bathhouse and a paradise of living water.

As with Jake, Stephanie and I have slow, easy days for intimate companionship. We sit in the shade beside the outdoor pool and reminisce about our walking journey through Vermont, Maine, and Quebec with her brother Andy. Four extended walking excursions into the Urique Canyon. So many camping trips in the mountains around Asheville that we can't remember all of them.

Once, while Stephanie and I camped at Rattlesnake, a small white owl perched in a tree like a sentinel to guard us through the night. The owl was unperturbed by the sound of our voices and laughter, nor did it flinch when we moved around the campsite. Late in the night, Stephanie shook me from sleep and pointed to the tree. The light of the full moon illumined the pure white feathers of the vigilant owl.

Early the next morning we began a five-day jaunt across the spine of the Blue Ridge Mountains aflame with autumn color, and scaled to the top of Mt. Pisgah with echoes of the white owl guiding our path through the rugged forest.

Two years in a row we hiked to the remote home of a Raramuri family nestled high in the cliffs above Rio Urique. We left the town of Urique on December 23 and arrived at the home of our friends on Christmas Eve. We celebrated Noche Buena according to their traditions by killing a goat for a special feast. Noche Buena is also Stephanie's birthday. A very special posada.

Recently Stephanie, her mother, and I sat together for the first time in over twenty years. Her mother talked about our history, much of which Stephanie had never heard. She was thrilled to put together so many missing pieces of the story and sit peaceably with her mother and father. We spoke without animosity or bitterness, yet straightforwardly and honestly. For the first time I apologized to her for my part in creating such a disaster for my young family.

"How we are now is the only thing that matters to me," Stephanie's mother claimed. Such graciousness was unexpected, and I cried twenty years' worth of tears. She is very much at peace with her life, giving much of her time in service to others and to her church. "You can always find things you did right and what you did wrong. It all boils down to what you are doing today, not last week or twenty years ago. It's all about today," she said, smiling. "I measure things on the outcome."

Along the mountain trails of the USA, in the woods around towns, the jungles of Honduras, and in the canyons of the Sierra Madre, I've discovered more about the way, the truth, and the life than a thousand verses of scripture translated from the Greek. Simple living and humble service have taught me how to restore my own mind and body. Paradoxically, chronic pain and debilitating depressions have led me on an extraordinary path of discovery above and beyond my wildest imaginings.

The experiences of my past walking journeys and those of my friends stand like altars of faith in my memory. Whereas once I turned to accounts of faith in the Bible for inspiration and guidance, now I draw strength from the word I've seen with my own eyes, living and real.

After many years of trial and error, I've come to the same conclusion about the Bible as Huckleberry Finn when Widow Douglas was reading him the story of Moses: "After supper she got out her book and learned me about Moses and the Bulrushers; and I was in a sweat to find out all about him; but by-and-by she let it out that Moses had been dead a considerable long time; so then I didn't care no more 'bout him; because I don't take no stock in dead people."

During my years of recovery, the fire has been my most faithful guide.

Several years ago, I walked for two days in a relentless downpour, the air just above freezing. I was drenched, along with my sleeping bag and everything else in my backpack. Daydreaming about a blazing bonfire and hot food, I spotted a meadow of straw grass glowing in the twilight, at the edge of a pine forest.

It ain't going to be easy to start a fire, I told myself, but the grass offered a glimmer of hope. I had a plastic bag full of dry stick-matches and a half roll of toilet paper. It's worth a try, I decided.

I gathered an armload of straw grass and twigs and placed them beside the fire ring I'd made with stones from a nearby creek. I burned most of the toilet paper and over half of my matches to no avail. I had been doubtful of my success from the beginning, but I was dejected all the same. How easy it would be to simply flip a switch in a nice warm, dry house and sleep with comfort, I reasoned, instead of hiking alone in a monsoon—muddy, wet, cold, and exhausted. I could hitch a ride back to Asheville … no, forget it.

With the strike of another match, a little trail of smoke swirled from the pile of grass and a flicker of fire struggled to life. I breathed gently on the fire as I fed more strands to the flame. Nothing else in the world mattered except birthing that fire from the soggy, wet wood. Flumes of smoke trailed through the pine forest. Raindrops pattered on the tarp. I leaned over the flame to protect my fragile work.

The little flame disappeared and the dark, lonely woods engulfed me. I wiped my eyes and rubbed my brows and bald head; fatigue pulsed through all my muscles. I wanted to slump to the ground and give it up.

Then, I opened my eyes just as a flicker of fire voluntarily reappeared. I leaned within an inch of the pile and eased dried bits of grass closer to the heat. The strands sizzled and disintegrated as others ignited and spread. The little hint of warmth renewed my hopes. I stacked thin pine twigs over the heat and layered more grass atop the twigs. Smoke flushed my face, burning my eyes to tears; yet spurred on by the possibility of success, I nurtured the fire with constant attention throughout the night until the embers glowed strong and sure. I was in a state of weary exhilaration, mesmerized by the beauty of the rising flames and the popping, crackling wood. Flames leapt into the air, casting dancing shadows through the woods. I danced around the fire singing songs in the unknown tongue until I was enraptured by the intimate presence of life—pure, primal, profound. Two days of cold, dark rain behind me, all my effort rewarded by this holy moment of oneness with the vital energy that flourishes within the fire and my body, within the woods and earth and rain and dirt. In the holy of holies, the very core of all that is life.

I'm strong in the woods now. I've learned to live with arthritis without it dictating the choices I make for my life. I can't remember the last bout of depression. The roots I sleep with and the flowers I pick from the side of the trail, the hawk, the bear, and the woodpecker are my scriptures, as are the fire, water, and air. The Raramuri Indians are my guides. My children are my best friends.

Steph says, "Amen, Dad."

Not long ago my son Andy organized a reunion for the men in our family. My two sons and I met my brother and his two sons at his house near Charlotte, North Carolina, and went to the NASCAR race at the Lowe's Motor Speedway. During the years that I had sought my recovery, I was most estranged from Andy. Several times he'd expressed his deep-set anger towards me, and I was well aware that he'd never forgiven me for being so absent during his youth.

We reminisced about my father and his passion for stock-car racing. Like my brother, I'd at long last been able to forgive my father for all the destruction he'd caused in our family when we were kids.

When Andy put his arm around my shoulder and gave me a hug, I glowed with gratefulness that the last unresolved issue from the dark years of my past had finally been settled. As with my father, I was able to grant full forgiveness to myself. Andy now has a son of his own, Daniel, my first grandson. I know he is determined to be a good father and break the chain of destruction that has been passed through the fathers of my heritage for centuries.

Stephanie's Epilogue

This is not the end, but a beginning. It is the beginning of an awakening amongst people who have the honor to cross the path of Mickey Mahaffey: to read this book, to journey with the School of the Traveler, to encounter a taste of the path Mickey has set for us.

For many years, it was hard for me to grasp why he would take this path. Was it really the only way? Why would he seemingly leave the "real" world behind? Many of the questions I had growing up were answered when joining him on his journeys.

When, at seventeen, I walked the state of Vermont with him to visit my potential university, when we lived outside for a month on the shore of Lake Champlain, when we arrived on the coast of Maine to pick blueberries, my questions were answered. When, at twenty, I lived in a small camp on the outskirts of Asheville for the summer to get a taste of "urban" camping, my questions were answered. When, at twenty-five, we went on a fifty-mile walk from Rattlesnake Lodge to Mt. Pisgah, my questions were answered. And once again, when we arrived in the Copper Canyons and walked the trails amongst the Tarahumara Indians ... all my questions were answered.

The answers are on the trail, watching one foot step in front of the other, sleeping on the ground, feeling safer in direct contact with the Earth than I ever felt before. The answers are found when the cloud of day-to-day life is cleared, and you realize that when you are in direct contact with nature, with the Earth and its people—there is the "real" world.

He has laid the path and told us his story. We have had the opportunity to learn about the legend of Mickey Mahaffey, this man who has been broken down only to be lifted up in the dance of the spirit. We have been touched in our hearts by the courage and conviction to give up what is safe and secure … to surrender to the way, the universe, to God—call it what you will. The only way to truly appreciate and love what you have is to give it up and let it go. We know what to do. It is up to us to do it.

It is with profound love that I write this as Mickey's daughter, Stephanie Mahaffey.

AFTERWORD

(The following is the English translation of the Foreword.)

To talk about Mickey Mahaffey is to talk about my soul.

When Mickey (Gringo, as I call him) and I met, I knew from the first moment that a deep and long-lasting relationship was about to begin. His outgoing personality, his eyes that reflect his soul, and his bright smile were just the door into meeting a man who holds the wisdom of life, the force of nature, and the passion of commitment.

Mickey's life is unique in many ways. He is friend to the trees and to the bears. He seeks shelter and healing in the depth of the woods, of the night. And although this is exciting because it holds a sense of adventure, it moreover shows an unbreakable will to remain in the roots, in the source of life.

This particular lifestyle, in addition to his contact with the Raramuri people in the heart of the Sierra Tarahumara, has made of Mickey a compassionate man who is willing to commit; to provide support, comfort, and guidance for those of us who have needed it. I believe that all of us who have met him feel that he was sent from somewhere better to share the right moment at the perfect place.

But to become who he is, Mickey has gone through a relentless journey of self-knowledge, radical changes in his life, and not few periods of solitude.

This is precisely what he communicates to us in his book—the path towards the transformation of a man who aspires to know and accomplish his deepest mission in life.

Throughout his story, Mickey takes us by the hand not only to know his own life, but also the network of human complexities: pain, emptiness, shallow illusions, but also awakening, healing and joy.

More than just a biography, Mickey's life shows us that the answers we are looking for outside, are within ourselves. That in our hearts and in deep connection with our ancestral roots we will find the peace, strength, wisdom, and intuition we need to be happy and fulfill our deepest desires.

—Nubia Yesenia Gamboa Rico
Chihuahua, Mexico

Manufactured By: RR Donnelley
                    Breinigsville, PA USA
                    September, 2010